John Habberton

The Jericho Road

A Story of Western Life

John Habberton

The Jericho Road
A Story of Western Life

ISBN/EAN: 9783744728188

Printed in Europe, USA, Canada, Australia, Japan

Cover: Foto ©ninafisch / pixelio.de

More available books at **www.hansebooks.com**

THE JERICHO·ROAD;

A STORY

OF

WESTERN LIFE.

"A certain man went down from Jerusalem to Jericho, and fell among thieves, which stripped him of his raiment, and wounded him, and departed, leaving him half dead."

CHICAGO:

JANSEN, McCLURG & CO.

—

1877.

PREFACE.

WHILE reading of the poor fellow who had so hard a time on the road to Jericho, two thousand years ago, I have often wondered what would *have* happened had not the Good Samaritan come along. Similar accidents have occurred when the Good Samaritan was longed for, but failed to put in an appearance; when priests and Levites passed by in unending procession; when the thieves had such an air of respectability that the victim naturally wondered if a reputation for honesty did not depend more upon profession than upon practice, and where the needed relief came finally from people as low morally as the Samaritan was socially. The true career of the person whom I have called Lem Pankett would be scouted as improbable if I told it as it occurred. It has therefore been relieved of some of its rougher corners and darker shadows; but I believe enough remains to show the risk which society runs in allowing the vicious to take care of the weak. I do not attempt to prove that the weak naturally fall into the hands of the wicked, for every observing person already knows that this is the rule.

If the religion of some of my characters seems of doubtful quality, the discredit belongs to the persons themselves, and not to their beliefs. There are few rascals, excepting those of the highest culture, who are entirely without religious sentiments, and who do not bend their best logical powers to the task of reconciling their practices with their beliefs. Possibly some of my readers—when they examine their neighbor's hearts—may admit that this habit is not entirely confined to scamps.

CONTENTS.

6　　　　　　　　　　　*Contents.*

THE JERICHO ROAD.

CHAPTER I.

IN WHICH THE HERO IS INTRODUCED.

"Lively, boys, lively! Trot along! 'Taint no time to try the turtle-step. While you're a-creepin' along like an angle-worm funeral, the Wabash is a-fallin', and if we get stuck way up the river, so 's we have to lay up all summer, and you have to hoof it to deep water, you can blame your own lazy legs for it."

The speaker was Captain Sam Bates, of the river packet "Helen Douglas," and his hearers were the deck hands, or "roustabouts," who were engaged in the operation of "wooding up." To the passengers, the men seemed to move with great alacrity, and the large pile of wood on the bank appeared literally to melt under their touch, but to the captain, anxious to get up the Wabash for a load of freight, and to get out again before the river, tempo-

rarily swollen by the "June freshet," should fall, the
men seemed to move as if going to church. Besides,
the captain had to say *something*—no western steam-
boatman in good standing ever imagined that a steamboat
could be wooded up unless some one stood at the rail
and roared encouragingly and cursorily throughout the
operation.

Again the captain raised his voice. "Come, come—
nobody asked you to go back in the country and cut
down trees and split them up before you brought wood
aboard. By thunder, I believe some of you are waiting
to have the wood grow before you pack it in. I wish
I'd have wooded down at Carrollton—there's a big cemetery there, and I might have hired a few corpses to tote
in wood, just to show you fellows how business is done.
Here! you slim fellow ashore there (this to a wretched
looking specimen of humanity, who, bent half double,
and with hands in pockets, was looking on), freeze in,
and show them snails how to travel!"

The person addressed undoubled himself, scrambled up
the bank, seized several sticks of wood, and hurried up the
"return" plank and aboard the boat so rapidly and reck-
lessly as to strike one man between the shoulders with

the wood, and to edge another off the plank and into the water.

"Bully!" shouted the Captain, as a volley of oaths came up from the injured men, and from others against whom the new man rubbed and scraped. "Bully! Now you're wakin' up, just as your work's about done! Lively, you loafers, or you'll be left behind! Haul in! Put it to her, Ben" (this to the pilot). "Cast off that head-line, there."

The head-line was cast off as the pilot's bell rang; the escape-pipes groaned like demons in agony; the wheel, astern, stirred the mud; and the boat glided slowly from beneath the overhanging boughs, and went staggering and trembling up the Mississippi. The Captain turned from the rail with the countenance of a saint, conscious of having done his full duty towards a perverse genera-tion, when his eyes fell upon the stranger whose perform-ances upon the gang-plank had awakened the spirits of the roustabouts.

"Hands not allowed on deck—trot!" exclaimed the Captain, when the man stretched forth his hands appeal-ingly, and said:

"Captain, let me go along, won't ye? I haint done

nothin' for God knows how long—been down with ager
—an' I've got a family to look out for."

"Well," said the Captain, looking significantly at the
stretch of water between the boat and the shore, " I
reckon I'll *have* to take you, unless I drop you overboard,
and I s'pose you wouldn't think that kind of me. Go
below and tell the mate to take your time."

The new hand reached the boiler-deck, and reported
to the mate. That functionary surveyed him critically,
hinted that the captain was an eternally condemned idiot
for employing so eternally condemned a rack of bones,
and instructed him to "go aft with the other roughs."
Having gone aft, the young man did not experience as
cordial a reception as he could have wished. The man
he had knocked off the plank upbraided him in scriptural language. Another man was dressing an ear which
had been wounded by a stick of wood carried on the
shoulder of the new man, and a gentleman of unusual
length, who was addressed as "Forkey," was bemoaning
the loss of a hat, his only one, which had been carried
away by the stranger's impetuous rush.

"Most carried my head with it, too," remarked Mr.
Forkey, in conclusion.

"I'm mighty sorry, I am," said the new-comer. "I hadn't no idee of doin' any harm, but I've had the fever an' ager ever sence I came to this country, an' I aint over an' above stiddy on my legs."

"Whar d'ye come from?" asked Mr. Forkey, somewhat mollified.

"York State," replied the stranger.

"What did ye leave thar fur?" demanded he of the wounded ear. "The West wasn't made fur blunderin' shadders to play circus in."

"I had to leave," said the youth, "to make a livin' for the folks."

"Yer aint married?" interrogated a gentleman in a red shirt, with a critically contemptuous look.

"No—I mean dad's folks," said the new hand.

"Old man hung?" growled "The Parson," so called because he was the meanest man on board.

"No!" exclaimed the young man, straightening and flushing; "and I'll try to whip any man who says he was. He was a shoemaker, and somebody got out a story that he stole, so folks kind o' stopped comin' to him, and he took to drinkin'. One day he was half mad with whisky, and went to the drug-store and ordered two ounces of arsenic, but the clerk gave him ipecac instid. Then the whole family got sick, an' the folks found some white powder in the bottom of the milk-pitcher, an' started the story that he tried to pizen the family. I guess folks is sorry now, fur he left town, an' haint been seen since—I reckon it wore on him so bad that it killed him."

"The family all lived, then?" asked the Parson.

"Of course they did," replied the young man, very quickly and indignantly.

"Parson," said the gentleman in the red shirt, offering the person addressed a silver dime, "take Slim up to the bar and treat him to whisky; he needs a bracer—bad."

"Don't you s'pose anybody else has got any money?" growled the Parson, giving the extended hand a vigorous blow which sent the coin flying forward to the boilers. Then he led the youth to the upper deck, and to the outer window of the bar.

The gentleman in red mumbled great oaths, and rubbed his hand until the couple were out of hearing. Then he spoke up hurriedly:

"Boys," said he, "that miserable little cuss musen't be tormented—he aint more than half-witted, I reckon, an' what wits he *has* got is pretty much shook to pieces with the ager."

"That's so, Baker," remarked a very hirsute gentleman, "and I don't believe anybody but Parson 'll trouble him, but *he'll* pester him to death, if he gets a chance."

"He shan't get a chance," exclaimed Forkey, the hatless individual. "I know Parson's mean ways about as well as anybody, an' I'll app'int myself an orphan asylum committee to watch the old scoundrel. I believe——"

"Sh—h—h——here they come now!" whispered Mr. Baker, and immediately the men, twelve or fifteen in all, tried to look as if they had not been talking about anything in particular.

"Where's the new feller to bunk, Baker?" asked Forkey. Mr. Baker seemed the universally acknowledged leader of the roustabouts, to whom was referred for adjudication all questions of dispute or doubt.

"That's a fact!" exclaimed Baker, looking around. "Who's got a whole bunk to himself?"

"I have!" shouted the Parson, quickly.

"Who else?" asked Mr. Baker. No one answered. "Your bunk's a top one, Parson," remarked Mr. Baker,

with hypocritical deference; "it's ruther rough to make
a sickly feller climb so high. S'pose you take in somebody from down below, an' give Slim a chance to save
his breath."

"I reckon," said Parson, with even an uglier expression of countenance than that which he habitually wore,
"I know rules aboard boats. A man's got to take his
luck. When there's only one bunk open, he has to turn
into that, no matter where 'tis."

Mr. Baker began to trifle suggestively with the cuffs
of his own flannel shirt, but the tall Forkey whispered in
his ear:

"I've got a top bunk, right opposite; I'll watch him."
Just then all hands were called forward to put off some
freight at a landing which the boat was approaching, so
the discussion ended without physical harm to any one.
The watchful Forkey, however, contrived to assist the new
hand long enough to whisper:

"Look out for Parson! It'll be first of the month
before we get to Cairo, an' then we'll get our pay.
Parson 'll steal yours—every dog-goned cent of it."

Then Mr. Baker walked aboard beside Slim, and said
in an undertone, "Keep yer eye skinned—that old cuss

don't mean any good—we'll all stand by yer—give him one between the eyes the first time he cuts up mean!" The new hand was considerably disturbed in mind, and his perturbation did not decrease as he realized how completely he was covered by the Parson's wing. The Parson seated Slim beside him at the table, and even helped him to food. It rather astonished Mr. Baker to see the Parson, after skillfully appropriating the best cuts of meat, as was his usual custom, pass his plate to Master Slim, and content himself with the next best cuts he could find. The Parson even sweetened Slim's coffee for him, which operation caused Forky to stealthily whisper to the young man:

"If you should feel bad any time just after eatin', go right to the clerk and ask for an emetic; don't do no loafin' about it, either—pizen sometimes gets into coffee."

Forkey climbed that night to his bunk with the praiseworthy resolution to lay awake all night, and, with eyes apparently closed, to watch every motion of the original occupant of the opposite bunk. This resolve formed a magnificent stone in the pavement of a certain dangerous but highly popular pathway, famed in proverb as paved with such material, for while in the midst of a

subtle mental device for overcoming the Parson, Forkey
fell into a peaceful slumber.   Waking suddenly in the
middle of the night—from a dream in which the Parson
was with one hand seductively offering Slim a cup of
poison, while with the other he was rifling Slim's pockets—Forkey sprang suddenly up and looked toward the
opposite bunk.   To his great surprise he saw, by the
dim light of the single lantern which hung in the ward,
the Parson, who was always grumbling about the cold
drafts which swept through the boiler deck at night,
folding his blanket double and piling it over his bunk-
mate, after which operation the Parson stretched himself
in his bunk with no covering whatever.   Forkey lay
awake for the remainder of the evening, determined to
be ready to give the Parson the lie the moment that gentleman awoke, and accused Slim of appropriating his
bed-clothing.   The couple arose without quarreling,
however, and the Parson was as kind to the green hand
as if he had himself slept under downy coverlets throughout the night.

Forkey pondered over the matter without reaching a
satisfactory conclusion as to the Parson's motive.   He
consulted Mr. Baker, but that gentleman, even after

stimulating his intellect in the manner peculiar to roustabouts, was unable to offer any theory in elucidation. In fact, when to have undisturbed opportunity for reflection, Mr. Baker climbed to the top of a pile of cotton on the after-deck, he himself received a revelation compared with which Forkey's was insignificant. He was lying on his stomach, as is the custom of the meditative roustabout, and his eyes naturally fell upon the narrow runway which had been left between the cotton and the side of the boat. Suddenly the unhandsome form of the Parson appeared, and, after dropping a roll of bills, quickly vanished. The startled observer sprang to his feet, ran softly along the cotton-heap, and reached the end of it just in time to hear the Parson say to Slim :

"Wouldn't ye like to have yer name tattooed on ter yer arm, so if ye got lost overboard, or got hurt ashore, folks 'd know where ye b'longed?"

"Yes," replied the youth.

"Go 'round behind the cotton, then," said the Parson, "and I'll get my things an' come an' do the bizness."

Mr. Baker, swearing eloquently to himself, returned to his original resting-place in time to see Slim start at the sight of the roll, and quickly pick it up. At one

2

and the same instant, the observer rose to his feet and the Parson appeared, saw the money, and exclaimed :

"Hello! found somethin'?"

"Yes," drawled Slim, his eyes opening widely; "I wonder who lost it?"

"Don't trouble your head about that," roughly exclaimed the Parson. "If it's anybody aboard he'll growl about it soon enough. Jest keep yer mouth tight shet about it—that's all you've got to do. Then, if nobody claims it, you can send it home from Cairo or Shawnee-town. 'Twould come in handy to your folks;—let's see—there's ten, twenty, thirty, forty, fifty dollars; bully! You can get eastern bills fur it fur about a dollar extra, an' jest think how yer mother's eyes 'll stick out—eh?"

The tattooing operation began, and Mr. Baker, doubting the accuracy of his own senses, speedily drank them into a condition of utter quiescence.

CHAPTER II.

IN WHICH THE HERO FINDS AND LOSES ONE OF HIS EARLIEST
ACQUAINTANCES.

DAY by day the little "Helen Douglas" gallantly
struggled up the great river, and day by day the mystery
of the after-deck grew more absorbing. The roustabouts
discussed in earnest undertones a subject which was
always dropped when the Parson came within earshot.
So absorbed was Mr. Forkey in contemplation, that on
one occasion, while wooding up, and struck forcibly by a
new theory, he with a shoulder full of wood, stepped to
the other gang-plank on which Mr. Baker was descending; the shock of the collision carried the wood and the
two gentlemen into the water floundering, in which
element Forkey unburdened his soul to his very profane
companion. The excitement extended to the firemen,
and from them to the engineers; in the natural course of
progression it reached the mates, the pilot, and the clerk;
finally it was noticed that the captain himself, whenever

the roustabouts were busy forward, stared curiously at the Parson and his pet.

The Wabash river was finally reached, and found to be more than bank-full; the boat might have sailed safely over the bottom-lands wherever the timber was cut away. A wicked thought struck Captain Bates and made him gleeful; he hurried up to the pilot-house.

"Ben," said he to the pilot on duty, " the river is way up."

"Rather," said the pilot, as he put the boat's head toward the western shore to avoid the current of a swollen creek coming in on the other side.

"Don't you b'leeve she could run the dam at Mount Zion, and dodge paying lock-charges?" asked the Captain, offering the freedom of his tobacco-plug to the pilot.

"Shouldn't wonder," replied the pilot, after scanning closely the trees on both banks of the river.

"'Twould have to be done by daylight, wouldn't it?" asked the Captain; "It's hardly a safe risk to try it after dark."

"Not *any*," said the pilot, with considerable emphasis. "If there's ever a time when a man wants to see the water in front of him, it's when he's runnin' a dam. We won't get to Mount Zion till about midnight. an' there's no moon."

"Whose watch 'll it be first thing in the morning?" asked the Captain.

"Mine," said the pilot.

"I'll give you an extra twenty to do it, Ben," said the Captain.

"Done!" said the pilot.

"Hooray!" shouted Captain Bates, spinning on his heel and rubbing his hands joyously. "We'll tie up at Mount Zion and keep up an infernal whistlin' all night so the lock-keeper'll be afraid to go to bed; then in the morning we'll shoot right along under his nose. Great Cæsar! *won't* he jump and swear?"

The pilot showed his teeth in grim approval of the Captain's wicked mirth.

From midnight until daybreak the gentle *Helen* lay at Mount Zion, shrieking and howling through her whistles in a manner which tormented the inhabitants of the town as badly as they did the lock-keeper. Toward daybreak, however, both engineers came on duty, all the roustabouts were awakened, both mates and the Captain

were on deck, and the two pilots lounged over the wheel.
As soon as it became fairly light the lines were cast off,
and the gallant little boat started on her daring trip.
Several miles up the stream the locality of the dam was
indicated by a great white mill on one side of the stream,
and the lock on the other. As the boat moved slowly
against the rapid current and decreased distance, a dark,
troubled line extending across the mill showed that,
despite the depth of water on the dam, there was yet a
perceptible fall; the same fact was also indicated by a
steady, sullen roar.

"All forward!" shouted the Captain. "Got to keep
her head down all we can, and there's no *freight* to do it
with. *Every*body forward—cooks, greasers, everybody!"

The roustabouts crowded to the jackstaff.

"Looks nasty, Ben," suggested the pilot off duty to
his associate.

"Yes," replied the sententious Benjamin.

"Must be a fall of nigh onto three feet—don't you
think it's dangerous?" continued the other pilot.

"Nary time," replied Ben, with a face sufficiently
white to give his words the lie. "There's nothin' to do
but get her head straight and hold her to it. We'll go

across as easy as fallin' off a log. It's time to give me a hand, now."

"Trim boat!" shouted Captain Bates. The two mates carefully disposed the men and the coils of rope forward, until the captain shouted :

"There! she sits like a duck!"

By this time the dam was but a hundred yards in front, and though it was only a wall of water about two feet in height, most of the roustabouts forward looked as if they would rather be somewhere else, if possible, while the colored cook and waiters seemed to grow ashy in visage.

A moment more, and the boat was within twenty-five yards of the black, roaring wall.

"Now—hold her to it!" growled Ben, between his teeth.

"Steady!" shouted the Captain.

The boat staggered up—she seemed barely to creep— she trembled so violently that her bell rang. Suddenly her head sheered the least bit from her proper course, which lay at an exact right angle with the line of the dam. The effect was seemingly out of proportion with the cause; instead of the water being divided by the prow,

and following the ordinary water-line of the hull, it struck
the hull "quartering," turned the boat's head still more,
burst over the low guards peculiar to Western steamboats,
rushed with terrific force along the main deck, snapped
the slight supports of the cabin, and caused the boat to
careen violently; in an instant the entire upper works
were carried away as if they were a mere box, while the
hull, with the engine still working, drifted down the
river.*

Strangely enough, no one seemed hurt. The Captain
and officers (there were no passengers) were seen
walking about on the convenient raft which the upper
works afforded; while the crew, having all been forward,
had been out of the reach of the water, and apparently of
falling timber. When the frightened men recovered
their wits, however, they noticed that the Parson was
doubled up near the capstan, and showed no disposition
to rise. Mr. Baker stooped, looked carefully into his face,
looked up, and remarked:

---

* Lest any one not acquainted with Western steamboat architec-
ture should doubt the probability of this incident, I would say that
I believe it follows in all particulars the story of the loss of the *Helen
Mar*, in the Wabash river, twenty years ago. Ohio river pilots
remember the case and its peculiarities.

" He's goin' to kingdom come, boys! "

" Where's that? " asked Slim, with wide-open eyes.

" Into his coffin, young man; if we ever get ashore to buy one," said Mr. Baker, very solemnly.

The green hand was on his knees beside the Parson in a moment.

" You've been mighty kind to me," said he, while a couple of big tears streamed down his dirty face.

" Think so, boy? " whispered the dying man, smiling feebly.

" Yes," said Slim. " Everybody else has giv me advice till I've been 'most crazy; but you've been a real friend—but I can't guess why."

" I'll tell ye," gasped the dying man, pulling at Slim's hand as if he would draw him closer. Forkey bent his head as low as he dared without seeming to listen, while Mr. Baker hypocritically pretended to examine the Parson's pulse; " cos—I'm—YOUR FATHER! "

The Parson's eyes closed, and a smile which a dying christian might have envied came into his face. The orphan, man as he was, commenced to cry audibly, at which Mr. Baker soothingly said, " Sh——h," patted the

youth on the back, and then walked abruptly aft, with
his knuckles in his own eyes.

The hull stranded on an island just below Mount Zion,
and it was proposed that the Parson should be interred
there. Mr. Baker, however, who seemed to have assumed
charge of the deceased roustabout, declared that he should
have a handsome coffin and be buried in a regular graveyard, with a genuine parson to say the word, and Mr.
Baker had his way. He was rather disappointed when
he learned that a fife and drum, to perform a dead march,
would hardly be in order in a funeral procession, and that
the only Mount Zionite capable of engraving coffin-plates
had conscientious scruples against engraving either "The
Parson," or "Slim's Dad," in lieu of a real name. The
real name, however, was obtained from the orphan, and
all obstacles to what Mr. Baker called a "reg'lar buryin"
were overcome. The procession was in appearance one
that Mount Zion had never seen the like of before; and
Mr. Baker and the orphan, walking directly behind the
minister, attracted unusual attention. When the first
shovelfull of dirt fell upon the coffin-box, with a hollow,
sepulchral sound, poor Slim uttered a pitiful cry and fell
on his knees, and all his companions trembled and turned
their faces away.

CHAPTER III.

DELINEATING A CERTAIN POPULAR IMPRESSION CONCERNING THE NATURE OF HUMAN SYMPATHY.

AMONG the natives who were drawn to the cemetery by the unusual appearance of the funeral procession, was old Squire Barkum. The sentiments under whose influence the Squire, who was the richest man in the town, had left his store in charge of a small boy and followed the multitude, were several. He was not devoid of curiosity, and excitants of that quality were so infrequent at Mount Zion that the Squire felt moved by ordinary prudence to make the most of every one which presented itself. Then the Squire was always willing to pray or speak at informal gatherings of a semi-religious nature, and he did not know but there might be some call for such service at the grave. Lastly, the Squire was human, and the Squire was shrewd; he knew that roustabouts sometimes had money, and that they freely spent it when asked to do so; he knew of the disaster to the boat, and imagined that the

men might have unusual need to replace lost personal
property, and that his shelves would be the proper place
from which to obtain the necessary articles.   How to
bestow a judicious word or two, not too cheerful for the
occasion, and yet not at all doleful, the Squire very well
knew; and he did not doubt that by so doing a few of
the roustabouts might be persuaded to stop into his store
on their way back to the river.

The Squire was doomed to disappointment, however;
the sobs of the orphan were more than his companions
could hear unmoved; so Mr. Baker, first tiptoeing up to
the mourner and whispering, " Come down to the wreck
when you feel like it," rejoined his comrades, remarked
" All aboard! " and led the party rapidly and *en masse*
back to the river.   Most of the native spectators followed
the retiring roustabouts, moved by the motive which
brought them to the cemetery; those who had come from
neighboring houses dropped away, until at last only the
Squire and the mourner remained.   There are some
natures in which the religious sentiments are excited
by trouble or disappointment of any sort, and the Squire's
was one of them.   He approached the kneeling boy, a
step at a time, as if he did it unconsciously, and when at

last Slim arose and turned himself about, he found the Squire immediately in front of him.

"You seem to have met with a pretty serious loss," remarked the Squire. "Was he your brother?—there's a friend that sticketh closer than a ——."

"He was my father," interrupted Slim, again beginning to cry.

"Father, eh?" exclaimed the Squire. "Well, that *is* bad—it must be very sorrowful. But there is one comfort—'Like as a father pitieth his children, so the Lord pitieth them that fear him.' Are you a believer?"

"A what?" asked the boy.

"Are you a member of the church?" said the Squire, translating his question into the vernacular.

"No," replied the mourner, wiping his eyes with his coat sleeve, "I aint seen much of churches, an' I don't know much about religion."

"It's a great pity," said the Squire, "for besides bein' for your everlastin' welfare, 'twould be a mighty comfort to you now. Was your father a perfessor?"

"A what?" asked Slim.

"A religious person," answered the Squire.

"I reckon not," said Slim, after a moment's hesitation, during which he looked far away at nothing in particular, " but he *was* good. You needn't shake your head—don't *I* know? The good things that he's done for me since I—since we've been together, are more'n I can tell. An' I would have been *so* happy if I'd knowed—knowed all about it," and again the poor orphan burst into tears.

" I hope his good deeds 'll be imputed unto him for righteousness," said the Squire.

" I wished he'd have stayed alive, an' gone on a doin' of 'em," said the orphan. " We might hev tuk care of the mother an' the children so well, now we was together an' knew all about everything, an' had work to do. But now he's gone, an' I've got nothin' to do again, an' I ain't strong or good for much, an' the mother ain't very well, an' the other children ain't big enough to keep her much—I wish somethin' would kill all of us, too!"

The Squire at once put on a judicial air. "Don't fly in the face of Providence, young man," said he. "God is very merciful; he might in justice have cut *you* down for such a blasphemous wish."

" Sposin' he had," exclaimed Slim, " wouldn't I hev been better off? What's the use of livin' when you can't be any use to anybody? Ef *you* was nearly a thousan' mile from where you was raised, an' was all to pieces from chills an' fever, an' worry, an' not havin' had enough to eat, an' there was somebody you loved needed lots done for 'em, an' there was nobody but you to do it, how would *you* feel?"

The Squire did not answer directly, for the simple reason that he could not imagine himself in the physical condition alluded to, and because, also, the desire to be practically useful to any one besides himself was one which he had never experienced except in the most timid and conservative manner. Now, however, as he looked upon the despondent face before him—a face none the less touching because it was so unhandsome and feeble— he experienced a genuine desire to help the orphan to accomplish the one purpose of his life.

"I'd feel real bad," said the Squire, "and I'm mighty sorry for *you*. And I'll help you—that is,"—for the Squire, frightened at the sound of so unfamiliar a statement coming from his own lips, was already anxious to modify the strength of his expression—"that is, I'll try to help you if you seem to be worthy of it—if you show that you really deserve it. What's your name?"

"Lemuel Pankett," said the boy, with a change of countenance that was almost happy.

"How old are you?"

"Nineteen."

"Hum—you're small for your age," said the Squire, "an' you don't look as if you could do much."

"Give me somethin' to try my hand at," exclaimed the boy, with such energy that the Squire unconsciously stepped backward and fell over the grave of one of the forefathers of the hamlet. "I know I ain't big an' strong, but I'll stick to a job forever."

"That's—the way—I—like—to hear a man—talk," said the Squire, fragmentarily, as he regained a vertical position.

"Can you take care of horses?"

"Yes."

"Make garden?"

"Yes—I always took care of mother's."

"Milk cows?"

"Oh, yes."

"Mow, an' make hay?"

"Yes, hay was the main crop where I come from."

"I guess you can't cut wood?" interrogated the Squire.

"I can, though," replied Pankett. "I can't do it as fast as some, but then, again, I can do it faster than others."

"Well," said the Squire, "I'll tell you what I'll do. I'll give you your board an' lodgin' for a week, say, till I see what you can do; then, if you suit me, I guess we can come to terms about pay."

The boy grasped the Squire's hand, and looked gratefully into his face, but the good man exclaimed rather impatiently:

"Never mind about that—you do your best, and I'll be your friend."

Whether from fear that the roustabouts would, missing their companion for too long a time, come back to search for him, or whether he wished to hide his own good deeds from his fellow merchants, the Squire took his new acquaintance home by a circuitous and almost secluded route. Then, while hungry, sorrowful, friendless Lemuel Pankett was dining in the Squire's kitchen, his benefactor and that good man's wife conversed together in an adjacent room.

3

"What you wanted to bring home such a shadder for, *I* can't see," said the lady.

"It is our duty to help the fatherless in their 'fllic-tion, the good book says, Marg'ret," the Squire replied.

"It says 'visit' 'em, not help 'em," retorted Mrs. Barkum.

"Well, he can milk a cow," said the Squire. Then, as his wife looked critically through a crack of a door at Lemuel, the Squire continued, "and he can make garden, an' mow the medder, an' cut wood."

"What have you got to pay him?" asked Mrs. Barkum.

"Nothin'," replied the Squire, "that is, nothin' for a week. An' I won't have to pay him much after that— he hasn't had much work to do for a long time, an he'll jump at anything."

"That's better'n I 'xpected," remarked Mrs. Barkum.

"What makes you say that, Marg'ret?" asked the Squire, with more asperity in his tone than became a model husband. "Do I generally make bad bargains?"

"No, Squire, you don't—I will say that you're the best trader in the county. But what could I think when you bring a fellow home with *that* appetite in the middle of the morning? An' then for you to go to mis-quotin' bible about it, too!"

"Well, Marg'ret, *t'was* a kind thing to do, now—that's as sure's you're alive. An' we'll get our reward for it. I meant to do him a kindness when I fust spoke to him, an' for a minute I didn't think about gettin' anything back. But you see t'was perfectly safe."

"That's so," assented Mrs. Barkum. "'Cast thy bread upon the waters, an' after many days it'll return to you again.' It's a powerful sight of bread, though—he's a eatin' yet."

The Squire looked through the crack himself, and remarked: "Well, he can't be expected to go on like that always. Besides, I'll set him to work right after he gets through—the potatoes need hoein' the very worst way. But say, Marg'ret, *don't* it make one feel good to do a kind action to a fellow crittur?"

"Yes, Aaron, it does," responded Mrs. Barkum, "specially when you don't have to be afraid that mebbe twon't come out right after all, as you do when you give a dollar to the Missionary Society or the Bible Society. Why can't he shake the carpets? That's a job that's been waitin, to be done these three months."

"Of course he can do it," said the Squire; "we must both see to it that he ain't ever idle. I'd feel awful if I thought I'd ever encourage anybody to waste precious time. There's one thing I meant to tell you, though; he ain't a believer—we must have him in at prayers, mornin' an' night."

Mrs. Barkum reflected a moment. "I don't see how he can do that very well," said she; "it'll break right into whatever he's doin' half the time, an that ain't right. Besides, I don't know 'bout throwin' away prayers on them that don't care for 'em. Nobody can come to God unless the Sperrit draws 'em—'pears to me 'twould be takin' the Lord's bizness out of His own hands."

"I don't know but you're right there, Marg'ret," said the Squire. "There, now, he's done—I'll set him at the potatoes at once. It's a wicked world, though; like as not just as we get him just as we want him, somebody 'll come along an' offer him bigger pay."

"Well, we can only hope for the best, an' have faith in the promises," sighed Mrs. Barkum. "There—just as I expected—he's helpin' himself to more bread and butter. I wish you'd gone when you said you would, an' put him to work."

"Another slice of bread ain't much, with flour only two an' a half cents a pound," replied the Squire, starting for the door. "I'm so happy over an opportunity for doin' good, that I don't grudge him the slice—t'wont take him more than five minutes to eat it. Folks won't think we're stingy *now*, Marg'ret, will they? I don't know anybody in town that ever done so much for a man before. We must be humble about it, though."

CHAPTER IV.

IN WHICH THE HERO IS PUNISHED FOR APPRECIATING THE
MERITS OF HIS BEST FRIEND.

DURING the month which followed the conversation
recorded in the preceding chapter, the good Squire and
his wife succeeded in so allotting the time of their
dependant that they had not the slightest cause to fear
that they would encourage him in habits of idleness.
Lemuel arose at five, made a fire in the kitchen stove, put
the kettle on the fire, fed the pigs and chickens, brought
in fire-wood and milked the cow; then, while the Squire
and his wife ate their breakfast, he hurried to the Squire's
store and took down the shutters—a task to which the
small boy, who was the Squire's only clerk, was not
equal.   Then he ate his breakfast, generally after receiving the information that Mrs. Barkum was in a great
hurry to have some potatoes dug, a chicken killed and
picked, or some errand performed.   After breakfast he
chopped wood with considerable haste, knowing that the

Squire expected his assistance at the store. Reaching the store, he received, weighed and stored in the warehouse such heavy or bulky articles—corn, wheat, oats, feathers, beans, hams, etc.,—which country customers paid in trade for goods; mixed in a mighty mortar, with a pestle, the various qualities of butter which came from the same sort of customers; weighed nails and other articles unpleasant to handle; measured tar; caught from a teamster the bricks which were being delivered to build an extension to the store; mixed molasses-settlings with brown sugar, to give weight to the latter; and when there was nothing else to do, white-washed the sheds, chopped wood to satisfy the winter demand of the stoves in the store, and dug at the cellar for the proposed addition. In the afternoon his duties were changed only as to their order; the closing hour of daylight was devoted again to the pigs, the cow, and the domestic wood-pile, after which he again went to the store and polished rusty hardware in the back room until the Squire thought it too late for another customer to come in; then Lemuel put up the shutters, carried home the account-books of the store (for fire-proof safes were unknown at Mount Zion), and went to bed. He never showed any indica-

tions of a desire to avoid work, and the good Squire and '
his wife seconded his industrious endeavors by always
providing in advance enough work to make it impossible
that he should be temporarily idle.

It quite naturally followed that Lemuel hailed the
approach of the Sabbath with a gladness which would
have been creditable to the most sincere Christian, and
that such time as he did not spend at church (about
attendance at which the Squire was persistent), was
passed in a recumbent position in the hay-loft of the
Squire's barn.   Friends he somehow failed to make; he
was neither handsome, rich, accomplished, nor eloquently vulgar, so no one courted his society; he was destitute
also of that useful social quality known as "push."   So
his spare time was usually spent in solitude.   Even then,
however, he was conscious of a longing that Sunday
might come at least twice a week—perhaps oftener.   He
grew thinner and more hollow-eyed than he was when
he came to the Squire, and contracted a stooping posture
when standing or walking.   The chills, which he, like
every one else at Mount Zion, had with unpleasant frequency, did not make it any easier for him to meet the
steady demands which were made upon his strength.

But the thought of the eight dollars which the Squire had agreed to pay him monthly, and which was to be of so much use to the little family of which he was the head, kept him steadily at work.

The Squire never ceased to congratulate himself on the steadiness and cheapness of his new assistant, and upon the truly Christian sentiment to the exercise of which he attributed the improved condition of the young man. When speaking to his wife of the profit which accrued from Lemuel's services, the Squire occasionally interjected a sentence which was religious in form and self-laudatory in spirit; when he talked with others, however, he made mention only of the religious and charitable feelings with which he regarded Lemuel.

"I hate to see a feller-bein' suffer," the Squire would remark. "It would be easy enough to have given the poor chap a dollar, an' made it all right with your conscience. But what's a dollar to a poor helpless feller like that? Like enough he'd have spent it for whisky, an' treated that whole crowd. What he needed was a home, and to be took out of bad company an' be taught to work, and have good influences around him. It mayn't all show out on him at once what I'm tryin' to do for him, but it'll tell. It costs money to keep a man like that, an' pay him wages too, so that he can keep his mother, but I'll trust to the Lord for my pay—this isn't the only world there is."

Such expressions were generally received by the Squire's auditors with that respect which is usually accorded to the utterance of rich men. There were certain sons of Belial, however, and not a few of the Squire's religious associates, who in the privacy of their hearts wondered how much the Squire would really have done for Pankett if he had expected his remuneration only in the next world. Not all of these doubters of the Squire's disinterestedness held their peace; the village postmaster and the Squire's principal business competitor—a pair of men who disagreed upon religion, politics, and public improvements—came into spirited accord on the subject of the Squire's treatment of Lemuel.

"He's making money out of the boy just as he does out of everybody else," said the postmaster; "I pay my man fifteen dollars, and he don't do more than half as much work, and yet he's a good man."

"Yes," said the storekeeper, gazing sorrowfully upon an ex-customer of his own, who was going into the

Squire's store, "he don't need to expect anything out of the Lord for that little job. By rights he ought to give some benevolent society the difference between what he gives that poor fellow and what he gets out of him."

"Societies be smashed!" exclaimed the postmaster, "he ought to pay the boy what he's worth. Why don't you go tell him so?"

"I would," said the merchant, looking a bit uncomfortable, "but 'twould be just like him to pay me off by trying to coax off some of my customers. Why don't you do it yourself?"

"Well," said the postmaster, starting and pausing as if he heard the horn of the approaching mail-carrier, "I wouldn't like anything better, but he's got a little mortgage on my house, and 'twould be easy for him to make me trouble if he took a notion to ask for the principal all of a sudden. But there's plenty of folks in this town that he hasn't got any hold on—why don't they give him a piece of their mind?"

The people referred to were many, for Mount Zion had a thousand or more inhabitants; they held substantially the views of the postmaster and the merchant, but the minds of most of them experienced sufficient relief from the act of expressing their opinions to their intimate acquaintances. Men who needed help and treated their laborers well, spoke of the Squire as a brute, and of Lemuel as a victim, but they never offered the victim the work which they had to pay some one to do, and which he was so able to perform. One of the Squire's official brethren privately informed some one, who privately informed the village, that he had been so haunted by that poor boy's face, that he had wrestled in prayer to the Lord for him, but he never offered the Lord any assistance in the work of remedying the wrong which he had so eloquently explained upon his bended knees. The Squire's own pastor was so moved by Lem's forlorn condition, that he made a special trip to the domestic wood-pile that he might speak to the sufferer of the Friend that sticketh closer than a brother, but he never approached his wealthy parishioner with the words of exhortation and rebuke which he had solemnly covenanted to bestow when necessary. The village doctor was firmly of the opinion that Lem could not last long in the course of life he was leading, and he said as much to the Squire, but when that good man anxiously asked what was the matter with his protege, the doctor turned coward and took refuge in a technical explanation of Lem's condition, which satisfied the Squire that *he* had nothing to do with it. One old woman, indeed, who had a habit of talking freely to whoever she met, unburdened her mind so freely to the Squire, that he wished she would transfer her custom to some other store, and he expressed his wish in vigorous English.

And still Lem worked hard and grew steadily weaker. The only practical sympathy and assistance he received was from men of a class which is not famous for improving the physical and moral well-being of humanity. These men spent considerable time in the two or three liquor shops, which were not lacking even in a town of so excellent a name as Mount Zion. Most of the frequenters of these shops regarded all varieties of work with loathing and horror; they were not devoid of sympathy; they recognized but one remedy for any physical or mental ill, so they showed their feeling for Lem by occasionally inviting him to drink. He never declined; the fiery draughts which he swallowed gave him nearly all the sense of strength, comfort and happiness which he experienced, and he soon learned to rely upon them.

When the Squire learned that his man-of-all-work was

in the habit of drinking, he was filled with righteous
indignation, and straightway summoned the offender
into his presence:

"Lemuel," said he, holding aloft the yardstick in the
manner in which he supposed King Solomon held his
sceptre when acting in his judicial capacity, "I understand you've took to drink. Don't deny it—Micham
allows it's so, and had the impudence to defend himself
for sellin' you the liquor, an' you for drinkin' it. He's
insulted me as I've never been insulted in my life before.
He lays all the blame on *me*. Now, was it to bring you
up a drunkard that I took you when you hadn't a friend
in the world?"

Lem turned pale, his knees shook, and he opened his
mouth and eyes appealingly.

"I see you own up," said the Squire, after a lofty but
severe scrutiny of Lem's face. "But I never expected
that any one I'd befriended would abuse *me* like you've
done."

"Why I haint said a word or done a thing," declared
the contrite Lemuel. "I —— "

"Don't you call it doin' anything for a member of my
family, as *you* are, to disgrace me an' my perfession by

goin' into rum-shops—the very gate-ways of hell—an' poisonin' their bodies an' ruinin' their souls by drinkin' whisky? Of course folks blame *me* for it—they wonder why I was such an old fool as to take up with anybody that had such faults in 'em, an' then let 'em go on in their evil ways."

"Why, Squire," pleaded Lem, "everybody knows you didn't tell me to drink; but ——"

"But you just went an' wasted your money that way, after pretendin' to me that you wanted to send your mother ev'ry cent you could raise," interrupted the Squire. "Do you call that the way to tell the truth to a man that wants to help you along?"

"I didn't think it was goin' to bother you," said Lem, "if I drank when I needed to. Its —— "

"Needed to!" echoed the Squire, with savage energy. "Well! I never thought anybody in *my* family would say they *needed* to pour whisky down their throats. But that ain't answerin' my question. Is that the way you're goin' to waste the money you pretended you wanted to send your mother?"

"I *didnt* pretend," asserted Lem; "I meant just what I said, an' I keep a-sendin'. I only take a drink when I need it.   Dad used to take a drink sometimes when he felt weak; and he never got drunk, neither."

The Squire shook his head, and seemed to go into a reverie.   "Your father drank, eh?" said he at length, as he raised his head.   "If I'd known *that* on the day that you buried him, I wouldn't have done what I did."

Lem's pale face flushed and his bent back straightened. "If you've got anything to say agin *him*," said he, "you can find some one else to say it to—I'll *leave*.   I've done the best I could since I worked for you; an' if I'd knowed it would have bothered you, I'd have done my drinkin' on the sly.   But I won't hear any man say a word agin my father—I'll thrash him first, or I'll try to mighty hard!"

The Squire understood the profitableness of discretion as well as any one; and, besides, he honestly enjoyed the contemplation of any displays of virtue which were unattended by expense to himself.   So he dropped the yardstick, assumed a placatory, confidential air, and said:

"Don't get mad, Lemuel.   I like to see a man stick up for his father—it does you credit.   'Honor thy father and thy mother,' says the good book, an' *that* decision is final.   But your father made a mistake—all men make mistakes of some kind—he made a mistake when he thought whisky helped him. 'At last it biteth like a serpent and stingeth like an adder,' the same good book says. If you don't feel as stout as you'd like to, chew a pinch of tea or coffee, but don't take to liquor. I won't charge you anything for 'em—unless you'd like to buy a quarter of a pound of either an' keep 'em handy in your pocket, in case you want to use 'em. An' pray for strength—*that* kind of help don't cost a cent. There— don't think any more about it. By the way, I agreed to deliver a couple of barrels of flour at the hotel before three o'clock, an' it's pretty near that time now. Be lively about it; you'll have to take 'em on the wheelbarrow, for there don't seem to be any teams handy. An' I guess you 'll have to get 'em out of the warehouse yourself, for I'm all alone here just now."

4

CHAPTER V.

IN WHICH CAUSE FOLLOWS EFFECT IN A MANNER PERFECTLY
NATURAL.

WHEN Squire Barkum repeated to his helpmeet the substance of his conversation with Lem, that excellent lady was greatly excited, and insisted upon the discharge of the depraved youth.

"It's always the way," she groaned, hastily swallowing a cup of tea to raise her spirits. "You take up these strange people an' try to make somethin' of 'em, an' you're almost sure to spile em.' I know my father took such a fellow once in Connecticut, an' took him when he was just a little boy, too, before he'd had a chance to learn bad habits. He made him so smart that 'fore he was twelve years old he could do a man's work at plowin' or mowin'. An' what thanks did he get? Why, that boy took to smokin', an' then he drank, an' 'fore he was of age he wasn't good for anything! You ought to turn

Lem away, Squire; he won't be good for anything if he drinks."

" Well," said the Squire. " I don't think 'twould be right to send him away to perish in his sins. As long as he seems willin' to try to do better, 'twouldn't be Christian to refuse him a chance. Besides, he's mighty handy—why, Purkiss told me the other day that Lem was worth *two* of his man, and *he* pays fifteen dollars a month."

Mrs. Barkum ate with unusual rapidity for a moment or two, and then she remarked:

" I wouldn't hold you back from what you think is your duty, Squire, but what I say is just this. Don't let's throw away our money on ungrateful folks. When he gets to be— Gracious!"

The last word was spoken with such perfect dramatic intonation and expression that the Squire dropped his knife and fork; he also dropped his lower jaw and started back in his chair. Mrs. Barkum unconsciously transfixed him with a stare, and finally exclaimed:

" Just the thing! I've got it!"

The Squire recovered his equilibrium and gazed enquiringly upon his spouse, who again exclaimed:

" I've got it!"

Then the Squire found his own voice, and remarked, not without a suspicion of petulance:

"I'm glad to hear it, Marg'ret, but you needn't hold on to it so tight."

The lady affected not to notice the spirit in which her husband's words were uttered, but she kept him in suspense for at least three minutes before she asked:

"Aint it about time for the next annual temperance meet—"

"I vow!" interrupted the Squire. "So it is. An' 'twont be *my* fault if he don't sign the pledge. Let's see—the meetin' comes off in about two weeks, an' I know the lecturer that's comin'; now, I'll just write him an' ask him if he can't put in somethin' to hit drinkers that's the only support of their parents—that's Lem's weakest spot, you know. But oh, Marg'ret, do you ever wonder why the Lord let's folks get a love for such soul-destroyin' stuff as liquor?"

"That I do," replied Mrs. Barkum, with great earnestness. "'His ways are inscrutable an' past findin' out.' There's one comfort, though—if Lem's elected to destruction, *we* can't alter the Lord's will, an' we can't be blamed for not tryin'."

"That's so," assented the Squire, "but we ain't to be supposed to work against the will of Providence if we keep the boy out of temptation as much as possible. I must keep him busier, so he don't get a chance to loaf into rum-shops—that's a clear p'int of duty that I've been remiss about."

During the ensuing fortnight the Squire displayed such unusual interest in the approaching temperance meeting that the committee, which had the matter in charge, attempted to secure from him a subscription auxiliary to the dollar which he annually gave toward the defraying of the expenses of the meeting. In this effort the committee was utterly unsuccessful, but the Squire explained that he objected only on principle—he did not believe in giving so much that other people would feel that there was no need for them to give. He was willing, though, to do more than his share in *one* way— he would give the services of his man Lem to distribute the circulars which were always sent out as final reminders on the afternoon preceding the evening of the meeting.

The committee accepted the Squire's offer, and the Squire urged them to have plenty of circulars. That same evening, at his family altar, the Squire returned fervent thanks to heaven for the opportunity which had been given him in which to let his feeble light shine. During the days which remained, the Squire employed his spare moments in tracing on a county map, a route by which as many persons as possible could be reached by the circulars. "It's a good deed, Marg'ret," he explained to his wife, "an' folks won't think none the less of us, nor come any seldomer to our store to trade, when they see whose man it is that leaves the circulars. It must be a good twenty mile—back an' forth, an' out—that I've marked out for him, an' it'll take him about all day, after he's done the chores, to do the job, but I don't b'lieve we'll lose a cent by it."

The final day arrived, and Lem, with a hearty God-speed from the Squire, and a pressing injunction to hurry, so as to be back in time to attend to his household duties before the time for meeting to open, started on his route. The day was hot, and the package of circulars was not small, but Lem started with a brisk step. He displayed a more cheerful face than was usual with him. The unusual nature of the labor afforded a pleasant change, and the Squire's remarks upon the honorable nature of the duty before him had touched a responsive chord in the young man's heart.

Towards evening it seemed evident that Lem had done his duty quite thoroughly. Besides the few people who always came from adjacent settlements to such meetings, the roads were full of a class of suburban settlers who had, for about the first time in their lives, received a circular at their own doors.

The Squire noticed the crowd, and was glad. The absence of Lem had resulted in the Squire's doing at his store a great deal more work than had been necessary to him of late, and a new sense of the worth of Lem, and a sense, also, of the greatness of that self-abnegation which had prompted him to lend his man to the committee, had not been sufficient to keep the Squire's temper at a proper degree of sweetness. As work decreased, however, and the effects of the circulars multiplied rapidly and visibly, the small boy who assisted the Squire, heard his employer softly sing,

> "Shall I be carried to the skies
> On flowery beds of ease,
> Whilst others fight to win the prize,
> And sail through bloody seas ?"

Looking out on the principal road which led to the country, the Squire noticed that something seemed to cause people to stop, temporarily, on their way. Several boys seemed to be standing about in contemplative attittudes and the Squire noticed that a woman was cutting from a roadside thicket some boughs, which she stuck into the ground between the boys and the sun, which was still an hour or more high. The Squire wondered what could be going on, but as the incoming people before reaching his store, turned from the main road and toward the church in which the meeting was to be held, the Squire found no one whom he could question. But business was dull at that particular hour, and as the Squire was entitled to a platform seat at the meeting, and was not, therefore, in a hurry to get to his supper, he concluded to visit personally the scene of the excitement. As he reached the corner where the people turned off, he caught fragments of the nature of comments.

"No use to try to do any thing with such—" he heard from Colonel Burt, as that warrior's buggy whisked round the corner.

"—An example to you, Georgie," came from the lips

of Mrs. Farmer Perry, as she jogged by on horseback, with her half-grown son on a blanket behind her.

"Some folks are nothing but animals; sympathy is only wasted on them," said ex-Judge Bowler, of a neighboring township, across his shoulder to his two sweet-faced, dim-eyed daughters, who occupied the back seat of his carriage. The Squire quickened his pace.

"—Infernal shame, but what can anybody do?" roared Farmer Bates at his family, who filled the straw-covered bottom of his great farm-wagon.

"—Good ducking—" was all the Squire heard, as two successful farmers galloped by on horseback, and then the Squire heard a man (from whom he had once endured some harsh epithets after selling him a horse) say:

"Let the old scoundrel that's to blame make the matter right."

A few steps further, and the Squire's anxiety was changed to sorrow and anger, for there, in the shade of the boughs, with his head on a pile of undistributed circulars, lay the Squire's man, Lem, dead drunk.

CHAPTER VI.

THE HERO EXPLAINS.

THE temperance meeting was exceptionally successful; the largest church at Mount Zion was crowded, even to the window-sills. The Mount Zion brass band was there and discoursed lively music; some spirited solos were sung by a professional temperance glee quartette; the lecturer uttered a powerful address, and though the Squire regretted that Lem could not hear the portion which had been prepared with special view to his case, he could not help being pleased by the dexterous manner in which the lecturer had made use of his suggestions. When the pledges were passed, signatures were numerous; many of the boys who had seen Lem lying by the road-side, needed no urging to pledge themselves to abstain from intoxicating liquors of every sort; while not a few moderate drinkers of greater age had been by Lem's condition so impressed with the possible results of habitual drinking, that their names appeared upon the pledge with a frequency which no one had dared to expect.

While the pledges were still being circulated, and just after a tremendous effort by the brass band, there was an unusual commotion among the small boys on the pulpit-steps; a moment later the form of Squire Barkum appeared on the platform. First whispering to the chairman of the meeting, the Squire advanced to the front and coughed impressively. The audience subsided into ordinary quiet, and the Squire lifted up his voice.

"My friends," said he, "I didn't expect to say anything at this meetin'; on any other occasion I should feel as if my feeble words would be of no use, after the powerful lecture we've all listened to. But out of the abundance of the heart the mouth speaketh, my friends; an' *my* heart *is* full, an' it isn't with joy either. A few months ago I picked up a poor fellow who was in great distress, and who I thought might be a proper and deserving object of charity. I took him to my own house, my friends; I fed him; I supplied him with money to send to his mother's family, which is dependent upon him for support; I treated him just as I'd have treated my own son, if I'd had one. But I found out one day that he had an appetite for liquor. I felt like sendin' him away at once, but that didn't seem a Christian thing to do; so I reasoned with him, and plead with him, and rebuked him, an' showed him both the natural an' the speretual way of overcomin' his adversary. I even, to inspire his heart on the subject of temperance, gave him his whole time to-day to pass around the circulars of this meetin'. But, alas! my friends, some of you know what's on my heart—a few hours ago I found that young man lyin' blind drunk by the side of the road. Of course I can't keep such a person about me; but I want to say, my friends, that I'll be sustained through my disappointment and sorrer if I can feel that my loss is somebody else's gain."

"It 'll be Lem's gain, sure as shootin'," shouted a voice, evidently disguised, from the gallery. A few thoughtless young people tittered, and suppressed emotion was noticeable even in the countenances of many citizens who had hitherto borne excellent reputations, but the Squire disregarded all these unkind manifestations, and continued:

"It'll be for the gain of everybody if they'll learn from my experience that the love of drink makes men evil-minded, an' thankless, an' unnatural, an' ungrateful, an' unmindful of the tenderest ties, an' ——"

"I aint none of them things," shouted a voice from somewhere near the door. The audience hastily rose and looked around, and those who mounted the benches saw, in the rear of the center aisle of the church, the short, thin figure—apparently shorter and thinner than ever—of the Squire's man-of-all-work.

"Drunk"—"Put him out!"—"Shameful!"—"Ontrageous!" and other cries arose from the audience. The Squire turned to the chairman and exclaimed:

"Mr. Chairman, I want to know if a member of this Society is to be interrupted by an outsider, an' one who's just disgraced this whole community?"

"Certainly not," replied the chairman (who had been a member of the State Legislature), springing to his feet. "No one but members of the Society are entitled to the privileges of the floor."

Bill Fussell, a rising young lawyer, and one of the members who had circulated the pledge among the audience, elbowed his way hastily to Lem's side, thrust a pencil and paper into Lem's hand, and then shouted:

"Mr. Chairman, Lemuel Pankett is legally a member

of this Society, having just signed the pledge, which is the only condition of full membership."

"He's drunk!" roared the Squire. "Is this meetin' to be insulted by such a piece of chicanery? Who sets any importance by what a man does when he's drunk?"

"Mr. Chairman," exclaimed the village doctor, rising to his feet, "the man is *not* drunk—I make this statement professionally, having had Pankett under my care for several hours. He has not fully recovered from the effects of the liquor he has drank, perhaps, but he is mentally in that condition intermediate between drunkenness and consequent mental depression—a condition which, in men of his organization, is marked by unusual mental activity."

The chairman again arose. "The opinion of Dr. Beers demands respect," said he, "and Mr. Pankett must therefore be recognized as a member in full standing. But the floor of the society is not the place for recrimination and personal explanations; Mr. Pankett cannot, therefore, be allowed to proceed."

Again Bill Fussell approached Lem, and a bystander with acute ears heard the young lawyer whisper:

"Apologize—say you want to speak a few words about a drunkard's experience—*then* he can't rule you out."

Lem jumped upon a chair, thrust his hands through his hair, and exclaimed:

"Mr. Chairman, I'm sorry for disturbin' the meetin'; I'm an ignorant man, an' I don't know much about rules an' regelations. But mebbe there's some people here that want to know how awful it is to be drunk, an' there's nobody in the room that has had later information about it than I have."

Auditors who had not yet stood upon their benches and chairs hastened to do so; one person of short stature was even so curious that he gave a silver quarter to a small boy standing on a crowded window-sill to exchange places with him. Lem continued:

"I made up my mind a week ago to jine the temp'rance society this very night, an' I'm glad I've been able to do it. This mornin' I started out to carry around the circulars of the meetin', an' just doin' that made me feel right happy—it reely did. I got along right well till nigh about noon, an' then I begun to feel tuckered out. 'Twas awful hot wherever the sun wasn't shaded, an' I begun to feel light-headed an' onstiddy in my legs. An' yet I wasn't half done. After I got my dinner I didn't feel as if I ever *could* stand up an' walk around

the rest of the way. Then I thought of how good a
drink of whisky would make me feel for two or three
hours; after that I couldn't think about anything else—
my knees, an' my head, an' my back, an' every part of
me just seemed to beg for whisky.   I'd told the fellers
at the grocery a week before that I was goin' to swear
off, so I was ashamed to go there an' drink, 'specially
when they knew I was carryin' round the circulars, so I
went in the back door of the grocery, an' made up a lie
about the cow havin' a lame leg, an' I bought half a pint
of whisky in a bottle to rub it with.   I drank some
as soon as I could on the sly, and then I got along the
road nicely, and didn't feel shaky a bit for two or three
hours; when I *did* feel peaked again, I took some more,
an' I went over every road the Squire marked out for
me, but the minute I knowed the work was all done
there didn't seem to be a bit of life left in me—I tried
to walk to where there was shade, so I could rest, but my
eyes growed dazy, an' I shook all over, an' the next I remember I was on the doctor's back stoop with my head
all wet, an' he a holdin' a bottle of somethin' awful burnin' to my nose.   An' if any body here knowed how my
heart was thumpin' now, an' how my face seemed all on

fire, an' how awful 'shamed an' good for nothin' I feel in my mind, he wouldn't ever touch a drop as long as he lived."

A perfect tempest of applause went up from the audience as these last words escaped the speaker—even the Squire was seen to clap his hands. Lem proceeded as far as "An' as to bein' ungrateful—" when the chairman rapped vigorously and shouted,

" Personalities are not in order."

Bill Fussell plucked at Lem's shoulder and drew his head down. "Put it some other way," he whispered. Lem scratched his head, bit his lips, wrinkled his brows, and burst out crying; subduing his feelings by a violent effort, he resumed :

"An' if there's anybody here, Mr. Chairman, that's got anybody else dependin' on 'em for a livin', I just want to tell 'em that the awfullest thing to think about when a feller's been drunk is, that besides wastin' his money, he's spoiled himself for a full day's work for two or three days to come. If there's anybody he wants to please, he knows he can't be fully up to the mark until he's got all over his spree. If there's anything he's got on his mind that he ought to do, an' is miserable until

5

he does it, its all the same—he couldn't do it if he was to die for it. When a man gets over his spree, he thinks more about what he ought to do, an' what he haint done, than he could do in a month of sober days."

Lem jumped off his chair, the audience gave vent to a storm of delight, and the chairman stepped up to the Squire, who still stood upon the platform, and whispered:

"He said it, after all, Squire—and he means it, too."

But the Squire was not fully satisfied. To have a speech—the only one he had ever made outside of a church meeting—so completely upset as his had been, and to have the moral effect of the speech so utterly set aside, was very provoking. The Squire mentally noted the names of such of the applauders as owed him money, with the intention of dunning them without mercy at an early date; then he said:

" Men *have* been converted to religion on their death-beds, an' I don't say it can't be done in the temperance cause. But I won't have suffered any less, and the lesson ain't any less to be remembered. But"—here a happy thought struck the Squire with such force that his rather uncomely face was completely irradiated by it—"but I wouldn't be a stumblin'-block to such people; an' as the

person that spoke last seems to be in earnest, I'm willin'
to forget all the feelin's I've had about him, an' treat him
just as if nothing had ever happened."

Part of the better class of people in the audience
applauded; others looked quizzical or doubting; while
from the boys in the gallery came the single expression
" Ah!" with an intonation and a volume that caused the
Squire to tremble and retire.

CHAPTER VII.

THE INNOCENT SUFFERS FOR THE GUILTY.

AFTER the close of the temperance meeting the newest member of the society hastened to his home. Finding, to his delight, that the milk-pans were full, that there was plenty of wood by the kitchen stove, and that there were other evidences that his employer had attended to those household duties from which he had been so long relieved, Lem attempted to retire and get some rest before he should be called upon to endure the rebuke which he did not doubt would be bestowed upon him. But he was unsuccessful; he heard some one at the front door, near which he must pass to reach his own room. In the desperation of cowardice he determined to escape by the back-door and spend the night in the barn, but as he opened the door he encountered the Squire, who had been to the well for a drink of water. His escape being thus completely prevented, he retreated abjectly to the kitchen, and industriously devoted himself to the preparation of kindlings for the morning's fire.

Mrs. Barkum entered the kitchen and coughed threateningly, sat down in a rocking-chair, folded her hands, stared at Lem, and groaned. The unhappy youth redoubled his exertions and prepared kindling for at least a week to come, but out of the corners of his aching eyes he saw that Mrs. Barkum's stare did not relax. Then the Squire entered, and Lem felt that the thumping of his own unhappy heart could be heard in the heart of the village. The Squire uttered the single word "Lemuel!" and the wretched boy's hat seemed to involuntarily slide toward his eyes, as its unhappy owner answered:

"Sir?"

"I hope you're happy," said the Squire, "now that you've so utterly disgraced us."

"'Twas the awfullest thing I ever heerd of," groaned Mrs. Barkum.

"I wouldn't have minded it so much if I hadn't been an officer of the Society," said the good man.

"And a justice of the peace, too," suggested the lady.

"Just so," said the head of the household, accepting

the amendment. "I believe in takin' up my cross, an' I've done it by lettin' you come back again, but the cross ain't a light one, I can tell you—" '

"An' its gallin' to the shoulder of *two* people," interpolated Mrs. Barkum.

"That's so," said the Squire. "There's no knowing where an' who it *don't* hurt in some way. The consequences of sin are infinite, an' there's no knowin' where they'll ever stop."

The Squire paused, to enjoy for a moment the contemplation of the possible extent of the harm wrought by Lem's wicked act. The silence seemed to the boy too terrible for endurance, so he essayed again to continue with his work; again the Squire exclaimed "Lemuel!" however, and the hatchet and stick of wood fell from the boy's nerveless hands.

"Youv'e signed the pledge," said the Squire; "'twas a good thing to do, but 'tain't enough—'tain't assurin'. If you could'n't be trusted to keep sober when you was actually engaged in temperance work, how am I to trust you when you're knockin' around at common jobs?"

Lemuel did not answer; in the mental condition in which he was, he could not easily have told whether it was day or night.

"I've made up my mind to this," continued the Squire. "As a sober man you were worth eight dollars a month to me, but a drunkard ain't worth anything. So if you want to stay with me, you must be satisfied with half pay—four dollars a month—until I feel sure you ain't goin' to drink again."

"An' half board," suggested Mrs. Barkum, but the Squire said:

"No—I'm willin' to be gen'rous, even at the risk of not bein' quite just—let the board go on just as it was."

"But he ought to work harder to make up for it," said Mrs. Barkum, and the Squire nodded his head and said:

"That's so. Four dollars a month won't be as good to your mother as eight dollars, but you can write her 'twas all your fault."

"Mother!" exclaimed Lem, springing to his feet and bursting into tears; then he hurried out of the kitchen and went to his own room, while the Squire said to his wife, in a tone not exactly affectionate:

"What *did* you say that about half board for, Marg'ret?—he might go tell somebody. Pay is pay, an' tain't no disgrace to get a man to work as cheap as you can; but cuttin' down a man's victuals always sounds mean."

"I don't see why it's any meaner for me to cut him down, than 'tis for you," retorted Mrs. Barkum.

"That's 'cos you're a woman, an' don't understand bizness ways," said the Squire. "It don't do any good to talk about it, though; let's have prayers—it's gettin' late." And the Squire read the parable of the Prodigal Son, a grateful tear coming into his eye as he did it; then he recited his usual prayer, with a single addendum to the effect that he thanked the Lord for again giving him an opportunity of letting his feeble light so shine that men, seeing his good deeds, might glorify God. Then the good couple retired. But a few moments after the light was extinguished the Squire exclaimed:

"Marg'ret, are you asleep?"

"No," said Mrs. Barkum.

"Well, then," said the Squire, "don't you see that if you put him on half board he wouldn't be able to do so much work? There ain't no economy in that."

"I don't know but you're right," said Mrs. Barkum, after a moment's reflection. "You *are* a wise one at plannin', Aaron."

"I do the best I can with such talents as has been entrusted to my care," said the devout old man. "I didn't think of that about the board at first, but when men does—their best—with what light they've—got—they're helped—to the right words by — the sperit of—" The Squire concluded his sentence in dreamland.

CHAPTER VIII.

THE DOCTOR GETS ABOVE HIS BUSINESS, AND DOES NOT ESCAPE REBUKE.

THE Squire had barely reached his store in the morning when Doctor Beers appeared.

"That man of yours was in a pretty bad way yesterday, Squire," said he. "Organizations like his don't easily recover from such a shock. I'm glad I found him just when I did, or I mightn't have been able to get him up so safely."

"You don't mean that you're goin' to charge your doctorin' him up to *me?*" exclaimed the Squire. "He's got to pay it himself. He's able to do it, he ought to do it, an' he *must* do it. I'd feel as if I was encouragin' intemperance if I was to pay that bill."

"I don't want to be paid for it by either of you," said the doctor, his face flushing. "I came in to talk about something else. Some weeks ago I tried to explain to you something about the fellow's physical condition, but

I'm not sure that I made it clear. The truth is, he needs to be taken care of. His physique was never a good one, I imagine, and he is now attenuated almost to a skeleton, his circulation is very low, and his vital force is extremely feeble. I don't see how he works at all."

"Ah, it's grit, doctor, *that's* the stuff that makes men. Think of Andrew Jackson, glorious old Hickory, with one of his lungs gone for half of his life, an' yet what *he* did."

"Yes," said the doctor, "but old Hickory, besides drinking a great deal of whisky, had something to stimulate him, some prospects before him, but what has *your* man got?"

"He's got his mother, an' brothers an' sisters," said the Squire, earnestly, "an' he cares as much for them as old Hickory cared for the White House or anything else he had his eye on."

"I'm glad to hear there's some such incentive before the young man," said the doctor, "and it explains what I couldn't clearly understand, why he has been able to do as much as he has. But he can't do it much longer. He's simply used up. He may last a month or two, but when he breaks down there'll be very little chance of his getting up again."

" Gracious!" exclaimed the Squire. " Where'd I better send him ? I can't afford to have him sick on *my* hands, an' there ain't any poor-house in the county. If he's in that fix, he ought to be savin' money to pay his expenses when he's sick. It's all very well to send money to his family, but he hain't any business to cheat other folks out of his funeral expenses."

The doctor stared—glared rather—at the Squire for a moment, turned abruptly, walked to the door, walked back again, looked the Squire full in the eye, and said:

" I didn't come to you to say what should be done when he died, Squire Barkum—I came to suggest that it would be advisable to prevent that catastrophe. He has signed the pledge and agreed to give up the use of stimulants; physically, that means that he will for a few days grow even thinner and weaker, and be in greater danger than he has ever been. I wanted to suggest that if you could lessen his duties, or change them somewhat, so that he would have less physical and mental taxation to undergo, it would be an excellent thing for him, by giving him a proper chance to regain a working consti- tution."

The Squire straightened the several curves into which

his back habitually composed itself when at leisure, raised his spectacles as high as the brim of his hat would allow, and replied:

"Excuse me, doctor, if I say that you're gettin' outside of your perfession when you prescribe a medicine that you can't give him yourself. It may all be just as you say—I've no business to doubt that it is, but *I* don't keep a hospital, an' I don't feel called upon to go into that business. I don't see why I should do any more for that boy than anybody else does; he does work for me, an' I pay him for it, an' that's the end of it. If he's to be helped, that's another thing, but my 'rangement with him's a business one, an' business is business."

"I thought I understood you, at the meeting last night, that you were moved solely by charitable feelings when you first assisted him," said the doctor.

The Squire winced, balanced himself alternately on each foot several times, and replied:

"So I did, but when I found he was able to work, it made things different. I don't give charity to ablebodied men. If he's goin' to die, let somebody else show charity, too,—there's no reason why I should do all of it."

The doctor's face grew fixed; he cut square in two a stick he had been carefully trimming with his knife, raised his head, and said:

"Yes there is."

"What is it?" asked the Squire, with a wondering stare.

"Because," said the doctor, buttoning his coat, "you're the only one to blame for his condition. The matter with him is, that you've worked him nearly to death; he drinks to stimulate faculties which you've nearly exhausted in him, and if he dies, you'll be the person particularly to blame. Practically—although you're innocent of any such intention, of course,—practically, you'll be his murderer if he dies."

The Squire brought his fist down on the counter with a crash. "It's a lie!" he roared. "That's just the way with you book-learned fellows—the first thing you find out is, how to shove blame on somebody. Here"— for the doctor was just stepping out of the door—"come back, doctor,—I don't mean that *you* lie, you *know* I don't mean that, but I mean I'm not to blame for any-

thing like that. I'm not to be expected to know about
a fellow's bodily condition."

"You know it now," said the doctor. "*My* conscience
is relieved, and if I hadn't been averse to meddling with
the affairs of other people, I should have said all this to
you long ago. Don't imagine there's any mistake
about it; the boy is barely strong enough to live, even
with good care. Good morning."

The fire that flashed through the good Squire's spectacles as the doctor departed, would certainly have ignited
that gentleman's clothing had he remained within range
of its focus. A bystander would have been frightened
even to see how the Squire's gaze rested abstractedly
upon a keg of sporting powder on the counter, as he
relieved his mind upon the subject of the doctor's imper-
tinence. He even declared to himself that he would
never employ the doctor again, were it not that he did
not think it right for so old a man to trust his possibilities for good into the hands of inexperienced upstarts,
like the other physicians in the village seemed to him to
be. But the Squire's anger was short-lived; prudence
was the leading quality of his mind, and it quickly
asserted its supremacy.

"I must make up my mind to *some* thing that'll look right to the doctor," said he, "an' do it quick, too, or maybe he'll go talkin' around to other folks about me, an' it'll be just like them to believe him; they all think he knows every thing about the way human bein's get sick an' get well. I always thought so myself, till this mornin.' 'Sposin' he should be 'right—only 'sposin' it—how can *I* be to blame, when I didn't know anything about it? I ain't posted on natural law, and don't the Apostle say 'without the law sin was dead?' An' how do I know the doctor ain't mistaken, any how? But this ain't thinkin' what to do to keep him from talkin'."

The Squire pondered long and earnestly; he pinched up his forehead, scratched his head, rubbed his eyebrows, and beat a vigorous tattoo with his fingers on the counter, but he reached no solution of his puzzle. The Squire began to feel doleful, and then, as always happened when he inclined toward melancholy, his religious feelings began to assert themselves. He stepped into his back room, where in his capacity of secretary of the County Bible Society he kept the Society's property, and took down a Bible. He opened it at random, as was his habit when troubled in mind and in search of consolation, and his eye fell upon the following passage:

"Add to your faith virtue, and to virtue knowledge, and to knowledge temperance, and to temperance patience, and to patience godliness, and to godliness brotherly kindness, and to brotherly kindness charity."

The Squire hurriedly shut the book. "That sounds just *like* Peter," said he, "puttin' brotherly kindness an' charity above faith an' godliness. If he wasn't an inspired writer, I should say he was in the habit of goin' off half-cocked an' gettin' things wrong side before. I wonder how it come to open just at that place?"

The Squire again allowed the Bible to open at random, and his eye fell upon this passage:

"But thine eye and thine heart are not but for thy covetousness, and for to shed innocent blood, and for oppression—"

The Squire closed the book abruptly. "*That's* Jeremiah," said he. "I always *did* wonder why Jeremiah was forever down in the dumps an' abusin' the Lord's chosen people. 'Pears to me my humble efforts to seek the source of ev'ry consolation ain't much blest to-day, but I'll try again."

6

The book opened and the Squire read:

" And Nathan said unto David, 'Thou art the man.'"

The Squire tossed the holy book across the room with such energy that it went through a window.

" Of course Nathan said so," said he, " an' very good reason he had for sayin' it, too; but I don't see what that's got to do with me. I should think I'd been given over to the adversary to be tempted, an' that he'd just stuck his finger in the Bible at these places. But I've no business to get mad over it—'resist the devil an' he'll flee from you.' An' its wrong to treat God's holy word with such disrespect, an' I deserve the punishment I've got for it—them window-lights cost nine cents apiece by the box."

The Squire went into the yard, reverently picked up the book, and again seated himself. This time he chanced upon the verse reading:

" So, then, every one of us shall give an account of himself to God."

The Squire mused. " That's good, clear sense," said he; " who wrote that? Paul!—I might have knowed it—Paul always had a level head. I don't know what would become of the church if it wasn't for Paul. 'Every one shall give an account of *himself* to God;' if that means anything, it means that Lem has to be responsible for his own condition; and so, of course, it means that I haven't got anything to do with it. I wish the doctor was here now—I'd just like to see him try to get around Paul with his new-fangled notions. I wonder if the doctor's really sound in the faith himself?—he got past the examinin' committee more on his face an' good manners than on his evidences, I really do believe."

And so musing, the Squire instinctively turned to one of the impretory psalms; this he read with great feeling, and remarked:

"Ah! David was the man, after all; he's the one for a troubled heart to go to. I don't wonder they called him the sweet singer of Israel, and a type of the Messiah. But even now I haven't found out how to fix this matter about Lem without its costin' me too much money, or else makin' bad feelin' against me. 'The righteous shall suffer persecution.'"

CHAPTER IX.

IN WHICH THE SQUIRE ATTEMPTS STRATEGY.

THE Squire soon learned that to satisfy the public was
not an easy task, for the public was more inquisitive and
less under the Squire's control than his own obedient
and obliging conscience. The doctor had talked; that
is, having known how powerful was the influence the
Squire could exert, and how provoked the Squire was
with him for disturbing the status of the Squire's household and mind—knowing all this, the doctor after recovering from the erratic attack of courage under whose
influence he had addressed the Squire so plainly, determined to fortify himself against the insiduous attacks
he expected. He accordingly told Bill Fussell what he
had done, and Bill told his legal partner. As Fussell &
Ball had never been called upon to assist the Squire in
the collection of bad accounts, there was no business reason why they should not express honest opinions on the

subject of the Squire's treatment of Lem, and they liberally availed themselves of their liberty and ability in this respect. The doctor also unbosomed himself to each of the Squire's business competitors, and these gentlemen, in exchanging views with their customers, alluded to the matter in that painfully non-committal manner which is above all others damaging to the person spoken of. The doctor's patients, most of whom had attended the temperance meeting, asked questions, and thus gave the physician an opportunity to say what he would, and the doctor improved it in so good-tempered, Christian-spirited a manner that his remarks carried conviction with them. From several different sources the story reached the Squire's pastor on a single day, and so forcibly aroused that good gentleman's conscience that he called upon his parishioner and administered some advice and counsel, which were not received in the spirit with which they were given.

For the Squire was not too blind to see when the period of conciliation was past. He had always freely admitted, in season and out of season, that he was conscious of the indwelling of considerable Old Adam, which warred against the spirit; now, he prepared to make a public demonstration thereof. To many of his fellow-townsmen it did not seem to be the first occasion on which the Squire had manifested a spirit which he could not hope to carry with him into the better world, and these persons hinted that the Squire was at his old ways again. The Squire interviewed his own lawyer, who speedily instructed the opposition; the Squire also laid his case before his own customers, and among these there were many who found reasons for taking sides with the old merchant. The case speedily supplanted in the minds of local politicians the famous Martin Kozsta case, which was then the most popular question before the general public, and it was argued with such industry that (as in the case of Kozsta himself) no one could find time to depart from abstract questions long enough to pay any attention to the original cause of the whole excitement.

Lem grew steadily feebler, as the doctor had predicted. All his duties dragged, somehow, though he never seemed to be idle. The Squire deprived the doctor's party of as many arguments as possible by keeping his man employed within doors, where no one could see what he had to do. He even visited him frequently at his work, carrying a pinch of tea with him, or telling a funny story, of which latter kind of stimulant the Squire had accumulated a good supply. But still Lem grew paler and more stoop-shouldered; finally he groaned from his room one morning that somehow he couldn't get up.

Then the Squire grew thoroughly frightened. He sat by the sick man's bedside, and enquired anxiously into his symptoms. He was ashamed to call Dr. Beers, and dreaded the publicity which might ensue if he called any of the doctor's rivals. Like most intelligent Western pioneers, he himself knew a little about the medicines required by certain physical conditions. Medicinally— and medicinally only—he had occasionally taken milk punch, with excellent results, and he longed to give some to Lem, but he dreaded the moral effect of the discovery by the patient of the nature of the medicine administered. Finally, however, a happy thought struck the Squire; he dropped a grain of quinine into half a gill of brandy, and by this means and the use of considerable sugar, prepared a draught whose principal constituent was effectively concealed, as he ascertained by personal test. This dose, administered three times during the day, was so efficacious that Lem was able that same even-

ing to milk the cow and carry in some wood. But the
Squire had no notion of undergoing a similar fright a
second time; so the next morning, calling Lem into his
presence, he said:

"Lemuel, wouldn't you like to see your mother?"

Lem stood erect at once, and the wrinkles went out
of his face. The Squire noticed these indications with
satisfaction, and proceeded:

"I thought you would; an' I've thought of a way for
you to do it without its costin' you anything. Sam
Reeves is goin' to take a drove of horses east this week,
an' he needs about one man to every five horses to help
lead 'em. I can get you the job of goin' with him, if
you like—he's under some obligations to me. The pay's
generally about twelve dollars a month, an' your board
on the way; an' 'twon't cost you much to get from Phil-
adelphy or New York to wherever your folks are."

Lem's eyes filled, and he caught at the Squire's hand.
The good old man was visibly affected, but he controlled
his emotion enough to remark:

"Didn't I tell you so? Didn't I say that if you'd do
your best I'd be your friend? Didn't I say I wouldn't
lay it up against you that you got drunk once? I believe

you've really tried to do your best, an' I want to see you rewarded in just the way that suits you best."

"Oh, it's just the thing!" exclaimed Lem.

"An' yet," continued the Squire, "there's folks in this town that say I've abused you—that I've overworked you, that all I cared for you was to get out of you whatever I could, an' then let you shift for yourself."

"They lie!" shouted Lem, ev'ry one of 'em lies, an' I'll go tell 'em so."

"Easy, Lemuel," said the Squire; "'taint right to show an angry sperrit to others when you're enjoyin' the mercies of heaven yourself. I don't ask you to say a word for me; it's my duty to endure hardness as a good soldier of Jesus Christ; but if you should find it impossible not to hold in what you feel on this subject, say it coolly, an' quietly an' firmly, as a man always should when he wants to be believed. An' you'd better say it soon, for there's no knowin' how quick Reeves may take a notion to start--his horses are eatin' up money every day."

Lem spent the time which remained to him in addressing every one he met, and telling them how good the Squire had been to him. So great was his earnestness that some of his late advocates were convinced that their opposition to the Squire had been foolish. Others, however, and among them the doctor, advised him to take the best possible care of himself, saying that it was no easy work to lead several horses who were without burdens, and were free to act as contrarily as the spirit which is charged with the tricks of horses might inspire them to do.

Sam Reeves finally got ready to start; he led his whole line of horses into the main street of the village, and most of the natives turned out to view the procession—even good Mrs. Barkum walked to her husband's store to gaze at the party. When the crowd seemed as large as it could be, and Sam Reeves emerged from Micham's grocery to take command, the Squire rushed into the road with a small shawl in one hand and a diminutive white paper package in the other. He approached Lem, who was tugging at a line to which several playful horses were haltered, and exclaimed in quite a loud tone:

"Here, Lem—you'll find it pretty cold sometimes at night—you'd better carry this shawl to tie around your neck; it won't cost you anything. An' here," said the

Squire, dropping his voice, "is a pocket testament—
I'm afraid you haven't thought to pervide yourself
with one. Let it be a lamp to your feet an' a light
to your pathway, an' may its precious truths make you
wise unto salvation. Remember you've got a friend
above—in him is no variableness or shadow of turnin'.
Seek him while he may be found; draw nigh unto him,
while he ——"

"TROT!" roared Sam Reeves from the head of the
column. The horse in advance started, and the others
followed; the leading-rope of Lem's line struck the good
Squire on the shoulders and propelled him violently
forward; a particularly merry horse snatched and proceeded to masticate the Squire's straw hat, another horse
gave him an admonitory lift with his foot, the Squire
fell; there was for a moment a confused mass of horse's
feet, Squires and dust clouds, and as the venerable ex-
horter regained his feet and hurried into the store, he
heard the populace respond heartily to the proposition,
"Three cheers for Lem!"

"Not a word about Lem's only friend, of course," said
the Squire spitefully, as he reached for a clothes-brush.
"That's all the thanks a man gets in this world for doin'

good. But say, Marg'ret, there ain't no danger of his dyin' on our hands now, *is* there?"

And Mrs. Barkum responded, "No indeed—'pears like a reel Providential interposition, this hoss-tradin' trip of Sam Reeves's."

CHAPTER X.

DR. BEERS GOES HUNTING, WITH UNEXPECTED RESULTS.

FOR a few days after the departure of the horse-party, some of the Mount Zion gossips tried hard to maintain the old interest in the subject of the Squire's treatment of Lem Pankett. They were unsuccessful, however; the cause having departed, every one's conscience felt easier. Lem was now beyond their reach, for either good or bad, so practical folks declared it was of no use to talk about him, while religious people, mentally confiding Lem to the care of the Father of all, felt that they had done their full duty, and rested peacefully under the influence of conscience void of offense.

Perhaps the decline of interest in the case of Pankett *vs.* Barkum was partially due to a new cause of excitement which had been growing with a rapidity quite alarming to owners of a certain sort of property. Railroads and telegraph lines being unknown in the neighborhood of Mount Zion, that virtuous town and

its suburbs became a very Paradise for horse-thieves.
This, in a country whose inhabitants were almost
entirely dependent upon horses for the service done
elsewhere by general machinery, was a state of affairs
not to be regarded with equanimity. The thieves were
numerous, active, quick in their livestock transactions,
and quicker with their pistols; they frequently intimi-
dated or bought up sheriffs, and they were occasionally
suspected of having justices in league with them, so
some of the most determined horse-owners in each
county formed secret societies, every member of which
was sworn to chase, at a moment's notice, any horse-
thief of whom information could be obtained, and to act
as judge, jury and executioner, in case he found the
suspected person with the missing animal in his possession. Who the members of these societies were was
seldom known except to the members themselves; they
sometimes went in masks, to hide themselves even from
their own neighbors, and the same masks were never
used twice in succession. Between the societies of
neighboring counties there often existed signal-codes,
and unwritten extradition and reciprocity treaties; suspected characters were passed at night, under guard, to

the headquarters of whatever county they were supposed to have come from, for all these "Regulators" professed to be and generally were law-respecting citizens, and conceded to every suspected person the legal right to be tried in the locality in which the offense was committed.

Dr. Beers himself was a member of the band which looked after the interests of horse-owners in the vicinity of Mount Zion, but it was not upon judicial deeds intent that the doctor rode out of town one afternoon, with his rifle resting on the pommel of his saddle. The doctor was an original thinker, with a greater fondness for demonstration than is noticeable in all thinkers; he was also an enthusiastic sportsman, and on this particular occasion he was going to test a new theory. In an adjoining county he had shot deer in a piece of woods not far from a spring, shaded by a large oak; he had done "fire-shooting" near springs elsewhere; if he rightly remembered the configuration of the ground, it was likely that what was called "Big Oak Spring" was the only place near by where deer would be likely to find water. They would not be likely to visit it by daylight, for the spring was in open ground, at least two hundred yards from the edge of the forest; therefore, they *must* come at night—at any rate, the doctor was going to test the matter to his own satisfaction. He even disdained the use of the " light " or " fire " which was generally used to decoy the animals, the big oak was hollow, the opening being toward the spring; he could therefore remain entirely hidden, and pick off his game at leisure. So great was the doctor's anxiety, that he started two or three hours earlier than was necessary; he therefore tied his horse in the woods, at a safe distance, crept into the tree, drew his hat over his eyes, and soon was enjoying that repose which physicians of large practice know how to obtain whenever they have an hour or two at their disposal.

When the doctor awoke he found it had grown quite dark, but the air about him was not so quiet as was natural to an empty field under the starlight. The doctor's senses were alert at once, and he soon heard human voices and saw shadowy forms standing and sitting about. The doctor's prudence restrained him from emerging at once, and he puzzled his brain to know who the men might be. Fire-hunters? That *would* be a shame; besides there were too many of them—two, or three men at most, were as many as ever composed a fire-hunting party. Emigrants? Perhaps; they certainly had horses tied in the edge of the timber, yet emigrants always had wagons, and fastened their horses near them; emigrants made fires, too, but the doctor could neither see a fire, nor the reflection of the light from one, nor smell the burning wood, which latter he could surely have done if any had been burning. Besides, emigrants were not in the habit of standing listlessly about. Drovers? The doctor could neither hear nor see any cattle. Soldiers? The Mexican war had just ended, and small parties of discharged Illinoisans and Indianians had frequently passed through Mount Zion on their way to their homes, but whenever the doctor had observed these brave fellows in bivouac, not a man could he see in a vertical position—they were either stretched upon the ground, or seated in a position which seemed to indicate that the principal duty of a veteran was to embrace and tenderly cherish his own knees. Horse-thieves? The doctor cast an agonized thought toward his own trusty animal, contracted himself into the smallest possible limits, and grasped his rifle. The doctor was not a coward; he had once—not intentionally—had a hand-to-

7

hand difficulty with a panther, just after discharging his
rifle at a deer upon which the panther, watching from a
tree over his head, had designs, and the panther's skin
now ornamented the doctor's office.   But between a single panther and a dozen or more horse-thieves the doctor
quite sensibly made a distinction, with the odds in favor
of the thieves.   If he only had one of those pistols—
new-fashioned they were then, and Eastern newspapers
called them revolvers—if he only had one—or two, or
three—of these, what a record he might make for himself—what a splendid practical education in bullet-
wounds he might speedily enjoy—what an unparalleled
opportunity for dissection!   The doctor was religious,
but he had a theory that all sins could be traced to
physical conditions; the worse the sinner, the more
abnormal must be the status of his vital organs—consequently, what a contribution to the cause of pathological
science he might make, could he only freely examine the
interiors of a dozen or twenty horse-thieves!

The men still stood aimlessly about; the doctor heard
their voices, but could not distinguish their words.   One
of them approached the tree—what if he should attempt
to enter it?   Why hadn't the doctor thought of this

before? He himself had on his oldest clothes; he might have quietly stepped out into the shadow of the tree, strolled carelessly toward the wood as if he were one of the party, made a detour to the spot where his own horse was fastened, galloped across the county line, not more than a mile distant, alarmed his brother-Regulators, approached this gang and captured or—yes, killed— killed some of them, and been at once the greatest hero of both counties. Oh! if that approaching man would only be guided away from the hollow of the tree!—the doctor did not hesitate to pray earnestly on the subject.

The man passed the tree, and the doctor prepared to emerge. As it was dark, and the doctor was a bit of a sentimentalist, he was not ashamed to kiss the cold barrel of his darling old rifle—he might never see it again.

The doctor peered cautiously out, and as suddenly withdrew his head, for he heard a shrill double whistle, three times repeated, and apparently from the road. The signal was immediately answered by some one near the tree, who twice uttered a treble whistle. Then the doctor understood that the men about him were "Regulators," assembled for judicial and punitive duty, and

that the prisoner was being brought into their presence.
Whether to identify himself, which he could do by
signal, or to be a secret spectator, the doctor scarcely
knew for a moment. He determined upon the latter,
but the men massed themselves under a portion of the
tree which the hollow could not command, so the doctor
was compelled to be satisfied with being a listener.

CHAPTER XI.

"REGULATORS'" COURT.

"GOT him?" asked a man who leaned against the trunk of the tree.

"Sure enough, Major," replied the man addressed, "but he's a queer case."

"How?" asked the Major.

"He acts as if he was looney—if he isn't playin' possum right up to the handle, then he *is* a fool, as sure as my name is Blizzer," said the man.

"Trot him up," said the Major. "Two heads are better than one, so of course eighteen or twenty heads are better yet. Let's talk it over together."

The man stepped out to the road, and in a moment returned, followed by three men on horseback, riding abreast; the man in the center had his feet tied together under his saddle, and his hands tied behind him. The men beside him held, each one, a horse pistol.

"Order in court!" proclaimed the Major. "Show the prisoner and the evidence."

Two men stuck balls of candle-wick upon sharp sticks, poured turpentine upon them, and lighted them; one then stood in front of the prisoner's horse and the other behind him. The other men crowded close, and looked curiously at the horse.

"Show light both sides!" exclaimed the Major, upon which the men with lights changed their position so that light fell upon both sides of the horse. Suddenly one man detached himself from the crowd and whispered to the Major. That functionary coughed, and exclaimed:

"Wait a minute, gentlemen—I forgot something. Take off your hats—hold up your right hands. You do solemnly swear, in the presence of Almighty God and these witnesses, to try this case without fear or favor, and strictly in accordance with the evidence? Now."

The men replaced their hats, and again examined the horse.

"Its Garman's horse," said one man, "I know him by the way the white works up in front of that off fore-foot."

"An' I know it," said another man, looking at one of

the horse's shoulders, "by that double collar-gall. Its
the only double collar-gall I ever saw—Garman *ought* to
lose a horse for usin' such infernally rough collars."

"Anything else?" asked the Major.

One man smoothed one of the horse's hind feet, and
exclaimed:

"See how he gives a little lift an' shake of his foot
every time I do that? Garman showed me how he did
just that same thing, an' asked me what I s'posed was
the matter with him to make him do it."

"Its the hoss," said one man, dropping back with
every outward sign of satisfactory assurance; several
others nodded and fell back.

"Lets see his eyes," said another; "Garman's was
wall-eyed—yes, so is this one."

"Did Garman's have any saddle-chafes?" asked the
Major.

"No," said the man who had expressed his mind
about Garman's horse-collars; "his collars ain't fit for a
dog, but his saddle fits like a blanket."

"Take off the saddle and the prisoner, and let's see,"
said the Major.

The prisoner was untied and lifted off. He fell

instantly upon the ground, while the guards covered him with their pistols. The saddle was removed, and the men again crowded near.

"There's no chafe yet," said a man, who felt the skin over the horse's back-bone just behind the shoulder, "but there will be soon; *this* saddle must be hollowed out of a log."

"Has anybody any doubts about the horse?" asked the Major.

No one replied.

"Now show up the prisoner, then," said the Major. (The order of proceedings had been in strict accordance with the ways of new Western counties, for in any one of them a horse is held in far higher regard than a man.)

"Stand up," said one of the guards, shaking the prisoner's shoulder. "Confound it," growled the guard, "that's just the way he's acted ever since we got him."

"Didn't I tell you he was looney?" asked Blizzer.

"Pour a little whisky in his mouth, somebody," suggested the Major. "Perhaps he's tuckered out; even horse-thieves get that way sometimes, I s'pose."

The whisky was administered; some of it found its way into the prisoner's nostrils, and made him cough

violently. This disturbance seemed to revive him somewhat, and he was able to remain on his feet after being
assisted to rise.

"Any one ever seen him before?" asked the Major.

"No," said some one, after a moment's silence, "an' *I*
don't want to again. He's more fit for a graveyard
openin' than for anything else, even hoss-stealin'."

He *was* a miserable, insignificant looking object.
Small, thin, flat-chested and stoop-shouldered, yet his
eyes were very bright.

"Prisoner," said the Major, "you are charged with
stealing a horse from a man named Garman, living in
this county. The horse is found in your possession.
What have you got to say for yourself?"

The prisoner opened his eyes and mouth, and drawled
out, as if soliloquizing:

"Just a floatin' along lovely, as if there wasn't ever
any such thing as trouble in the world. I wish everybody I knowed could be so happy."

"What did I tell you?" said Blizzer, spinning about
on his heels and appealing to every one.

"Playing crazy is a losin' game here, prisoner," said
the Major. "We've seen it played before."

"Play?" exclaimed the prisoner. "Oh, it's just like as if I was a little boy again, 'fore I ever knowed what trouble was. I feel just as happy as if I was playin' all the time."

"Show him the rope," growled some one in the Major's ear—"*that'll* bring out the truth if he's tryin' to gum us."

"The evidence is all against you, prisoner," said the Major, sternly, "and there's only one punishment. Say your prayers. Men, do your duty."

The guards lifted the prisoner upon the horse, still unsaddled; the prisoner was seated with his back to the horse's head. The prisoner was humming a tune softly, when his eye caught sight of a rope which was being thrown across a bough of the tree. He stared and stopped humming; he looked about him with a start, as if awaking from a sleep, and screamed:

"Mother!"

Half a dozen double whistles shrilly uttered, pierced the air. Every one started and into the midst of the crowd burst the doctor.

"Excuse me gentlemen — I'm Doctor Beers — next county. Lem—Lem, you poor old fellow, what does all this mean?"

Lem did not answer; he had already fallen from the horse. The doctor was by his side in an instant, and had his finger on Lem's pulse.

"Show light here a moment?" asked the doctor. Both men with lights approached the doctor, and so did every one else. The doctor looked into Lem's half-opened eyes, observed his face closely, and finally exclaimed:

"I know this man well, gentlemen, and don't believe there's a more harmless person in the world. The trouble with him *now* is that he is almost dead. He has a severe malarial fever, and is delirious under its influence, and this shock will probably take him off. I do wish I'd come out of that tree in time to prevent it, but I had no idea who your prisoner was, and I didn't wish to intrude."

"That's all very well, doctor," said the Major, "but what we want to know is, how did he get Garman's horse?"

"Wait until he gets well," said the doctor, "and you can probably find out—you certainly can't while he's in this condition. I know his constitution, gentlemen. Weeks ago I warned his employer that he would die soon if he wasn't better cared for. He may die now, within ten minutes—in fact, it'll be strange if he don't."

" And not confess or tell who else is in his gang?" exclaimed the Major. " Thunder! try the whisky on him again, boys—that'll bring him to long enough to own up or explain."

The man with the whisky-bottle approached; the doctor snatched the bottle and threw it away. An angry murmur ran through the crowd; and several sets of earnest arguments began at once, when suddenly every sound was hushed by a deep voice which exclaimed:

" What are you doing to that man?"

Everybody looked in the direction from which the voice came, and they beheld a large man on a large horse. The man seemed to be a stranger, for no one greeted him by name; every one seemed to be busy wondering how he had approached without being heard.

" What are you doing to that man?" the stranger repeated.

The Major threw up his hat-brim a little way, folded his arms, and said:

" I don't know as its any of your business, but we like to be accommodating. We were about to hang him for stealing Garman's horse, but he seems to have fainted.

We thought we'd like to find out first, though, how he came by the animal."

"Well, *I* can tell you that," said the stranger. "He was turned off by Sam Reeves a couple of days ago for being used up, an' not fit to lead horses, an' he was tryin' to walk back to Mount Zion, where he had friends. I met him on the road, an' he was the most pitiful sight I ever *did* see, all burnin' up with fever. I hadn't any time to lose, but every once in a while he'd quit whatever he was sayin' an' cry out 'Mother!' in a way that went right through me. I've got a mother myself, an' his hollerin' was too much for me, so I got off my hoss, an' helped him onto him, an' told him to ride to Mount Zion as fast as the Lord would let him."

"And where did *you* get Garman's horse, may I enquire?" said the Major.

The stranger gathered his bridle-reins tightly, turned his horse's head a trifle, shouted "Stole him!" and galloped off.

Every one stared, except the Major; but that gentleman snatched a pistol from one of the guards and fired; the horse-thief groaned and fell from his horse. The Regulators abandoned Lem, and the doctor followed them, thinking, perhaps, that an ever-kind Providence was about to compensate him for that disappointment about examining bullet-wounds and dissecting horse-thieves.

"I'm a goner!" gasped the thief; "but 'tain't as bad as it might have been, if I hadn't saved that poor little cuss."

The doctor examined the man's wounds, but the Major scrutinized the backs of the desperado's hands, and then removed his hat and looked curiously at his left temple.

"It's Bill Hixton, boys!" he exclaimed. "Every mark's according to description. I guess we haven't made such a bad night's work, after all."

An hour later Bill Hixton, who the doctor thought might recover, was safe in the county jail; while the doctor, unable to borrow a horse from any one, took Lem on his own and walked, leading the horse, to Mount Zion.

CHAPTER XII.

THE RIGHTEOUS SHALL SUFFER PERSECUTION.

The morning sun shone brightly into Mrs. Barkum's tidy kitchen, and its cheery influence was materially assisted by the blazing fire, which a sharp November morning necessitated in the large fire-place. Wood was cheap at Mount Zion; even the most dilatory of the Squire's debtors were willing to reduce their accounts by depositing cord-wood in the Squire's back-yard, and the fire-place was wide enough to receive the wood in the lengths in which it was delivered. At one side of the fire-place stooped Mrs. Barkum, frying sausages, and occasionally looking into a Dutch oven, from which came an odor of corn-bread, not unmixed with that of saleratus; at the other side sat the Squire, who, while waiting for his breakfast, was improving the fleeting moments by perusing the family Bible. Both seemed too busily engaged to enter into conversation, but finally the Squire remarked:

"Marg'ret, I sometimes think we're never half thankful enough that things ain't as they used to be in the time of Christ."

Mrs. Barkum paused in the act of turning a fine juicy sausage; she stared at the Squire so steadily that the sausage glided gently off her fork into the fire, as the good old woman exclaimed:

"Squire, what on earth *do* you mean? I hope you ain't backslidin'."

"Oh, Marg'ret," groaned the Squire, "of course I ain't. You must have got out of the wrong side of the bed this mornin'. I've just been readin' about the man that went down from Jerusalem unto Jericho, an' fell ——"

"Oh!" said Mrs. Barkum, "I didn't understand you. You might have put it plainer, though, an' not give me such a fright. That was the very biggest one of them sassiges, too."

"Can't you save it yet, for Lem?" said the Squire. "Sho! I keep forgettin' he ain't here no more. Poor feller—I hope he'll find his Saviour before he dies. But just think how 'twould be if a man couldn't go between towns nowadays without bein' robbed. Business must have been mighty uncertain in those days."

"Like enough," said Mrs. Barkum, hastily withdrawing from the coals the coffee-pot, which was boiling over.

"Human nature was meaner then than 'tis now, too," continued the Squire. "Think of that priest an' Levite lettin' that poor fellow suffer, when it only cost the good Samaritan a penny to relieve his necessity. To be sure I've heard ministers explain that the penny of those days was as good as thirty cents now, but I wouldn't have grudged thirty cents to keep a man out of trouble, 'pears to me."

"I should think not," said Mrs. Barkum, as she proceeded to put the breakfast on the table. "Think of how much you done for Lem."

"Yes," said the Squire, "but I got my reward. Think of what 'twould have cost me if he died on my hands— we can never be thankful enough that we was saved from that. Let's ask a blessin'."

The two old heads bowed reverently, and then were suddenly uplifted, for a hand was heard at the door-latch. A second later the door opened, and Lem staggered in and dropped into a chair by the fire-place.

The Squire sprang up and groaned; Mrs. Barkum

8

turned in her chair and sighed. The Squire soon recovered sufficiently from his surprise to sternly exclaim:

"Lemuel! what does this mean?"

"I feel as if I was goin' to die," Lem feebly replied. Then Mrs. Barkum arose and exclaimed:

"Squire, somethin' must be done at once!"

"Thank you, Miss Barkum," said Lem. "I need it, I do assure you."

"You're a—" began Mrs. Barkum, when her husband interrupted her by saying hurriedly:

"This way a minute, Marg'ret."

The venerable couple stepped into an adjoining room, and looked each other squarely in the face. The good Squire's face was full of trouble, and his wife's was full of anger.

"He ain't to die *here*, anyhow," gasped Mrs. Barkum at last.

"Of course he ain't," whispered the Squire; "but let's think up some way to manage it decently."

"I've been a-promisin' for better 'n five year to go see my sister at Evansville, an' now my heart's set on goin' by this mornin's stage," said Mrs. Barkum. "The washin's done, and I can get ready in half an hour."

"You're a good wife, Marg'ret," said the Squire with great earnestness. "'The heart of her husband doth safely trust in her!' as the good book says. Wait a minute—he must have money by him yet—I'll go right out an' look for a boardin' place for him. Ben Ringsell takes boarders cheap, an' its our duty to see that Lem don't pay more than he'd ought to."

"Mebbe he hain't got enough money to take care of him till—till he finds out whether he lives, an' then they'll come down on you for it," said Mrs. Barkum.

The Squire smiled condescendingly. "That's all you women know about business," said he. "You don't s'pose *I* engage his board, do you? I'll tell 'em *he* wants to get a boardin' place, as he's pretty poorly, an' that he's got the money to pay for it. I'll just see *if* he's got it, though."

The Squire learned that Lem still had some money. He explained that Mrs. Barkum had arranged to go to Evansville by the stage of that morning; he was authorized by Lem to engage board for him, he engaged the board accordingly, and moved Lem to his new quarters with such celerity that when, at noon, Dr. Beers called to see his patient, he found the house tightly locked, and was obliged to drive to the Squire's store for further information.

"No," said the Squire, "he isn't a pauper, an' he's got a spirit of his own. He's got money in his pocket, an' he's man enough to want to take care of himself. Grit, doctor—didn't I tell you so, months ago."

When the doctor's story of Lem's narrow escape went the rounds, Mount Zion was worked up to a fever heat of feeling. The Squire's pastor alluded to the matter in prayer-meeting, and made it the subject of a powerful discourse upon special interpositions of Providence. Ben Ringsell's daughter was summoned to the front door one morning, to receive for the sick man an elegant sponge-cake, sent by Mrs. Berrington, who was so aristocratic that she kept two servants. On the same day the town butcher called with steak enough to feed a large family; 'twas for the sick man, he said, and 'twas all tenderloin, too. The teacher of the girls' Bible class in the Sunday School attached to the Squire's own church— a refined, sensitive woman—sent Lem a bottle of Florida Water, which was then the rarest perfumery known at the Mount Zion drug store. Ijam Fielder, a good-for-nothing mulatto, who spent most of his time hunting, left a splendid assortment of game for Lem, with the word that whenever Lem would like to hear a fiddle played by a man that knew how, he would like to be sent for. Saintly old Aunty Bates, who, with a slender purse but a great warm heart, managed to help every one who was in trouble, went straightway to work to knit Lem some warm stockings to wear when he recovered, as she hoped and prayed he might. The Smith girls, who alone among the Mount Zion ladies boasted that they never worked, compounded a custard with their own fair hands, and delivered it in person, lest its appearance should be marred by a careless bearer. And one evening Dr. Beers was closely questioned by Micham, keeper of the liquor shop, and had pressed upon him, for Lem's especial use and benefit, a flask of brandy, which Micham declared could not be equalled west of the Alleghanies.

CHAPTER XIII.

PRIESTS AND LEVITES.

DURING the fortnight in which it seemed doubtful whether Lem Pankett would recover, he was the principal subject of conversation at Mount Zion, and every one agreed that the Squire displayed his naturally mean spirit by not taking the sick man in his own house, and seeing to it that he was decently buried. Every one told every one else what *they* would have done, had Lem been a faithful employe of their own. There were even many who declared that even if Lem had been a nigger, and the circumstances been still the same, they should have cared for him under their own roofs. This, from people who lived within a few miles of a slave State, and before an abolition party openly existed in the West, was as strong language as the most earnest humanitarian could desire.

When, however, Dr. Beers announced, with pardonable pride, that although Lem had been very dangerously ill, he was now in a fair way to recover, the direction of conversation was somewhat changed. It now became the task—not at all hard—for each man to convince his neighbor that it was the Squire's duty to again find occupation for Lem. A self-appointed committee of one waited on the Squire, and informally expressed the sense of the public, but the Squire vigorously declined to be guided thereby.

"The doctor says he isn't fit to work much," said he, "an, I don't employ men to stand around an' hold themselves up. I ain't without charity, but I'm not the man to take the whole charge of the only object of charity in the county. The right place for him is the town where he came from, an' where his people have contributted, by payin' taxes to the public fund that's drawn on for the support of the poor. I've done more for him than anybody else in town; to be sure, the doctor's made him well, but he's doctored him in time that he wouldn't have been doin' anything else in, and I don't s'pose all the medicines he give him ever cost a dollar. *I* took him when he hadn't a friend; I kept him a week for nothin'; I held onto him when I'd have been justified in sendin' him away; I put myself out to find him a way of gettin' back to his mother when he wanted to go; I gave him a shawl to keep himself warm with—I've done *lots* of things for him. He's of age,—he's come back here of his own free will; *he* don't want to live on any body else;—why don't somebody give him work, if they think so much of him? *I'd* do it quick enough if he was strong enough to do what's got to be done, but the pork-packin' an' corn-shellin' season's nearly on us, an' I've got to have a strong man that ain't likely to get sick an' upset all my business calculations."

The Squire said as much to Lem, though in a kinder manner, and with sundry quotations of Scripture, on the first day when the convalescent lounged into the store. Lem admitted the wisdom of the Squire's remarks; and was as grateful when the Squire promised to " keep him in mind if he heard of anything turnin' up "—as if the Squire meant more by that expression than other people do under similar circumstances.

Then began for Lem a course of experience through which thousands of men have passed, and thousands are all the while passing, but which, in spite of its common-ness, is full of tortures keener than any that Christian zealot or heathen executioner were ever able to devise—a course of experience whose influence upon character, and, through character, upon the world—the usual nature of religious teaching has never succeeded in overcoming. No one spoke unkindly to Lem, but no one greeted him with any cordiality. Business men did not frown when he approached, but, no matter how great their leisure might be, they never gave him any encouragement to enlarge upon his necessity for employment. Occasionally some one would quiet his own conscience and get rid of Lem by giving him a dollar, or some smaller coin, and then intimate by his tone and action that his entire duty was done. Others, equally practical but not willing to pay so large a price for a peaceful mind, would give Lem employment for an hour or two, and pay him at the current rate of daily labor; still others would feel that they had discharged all their moral obligation by giving Lem a full meal.

And yet the people of Mount Zion were as good, collectively, as those of any other town, and better than those of many, for Mount Zion was originally a religious colony, and the descendants of the founders were people of considerable character. Every one was sorry for Lem —every one but Lem himself heard everywhere what an unfortunate but deserving fellow he was. As Lem strolled aimlessly past Mrs. Berrington's house one afternoon, while that lady was entertaining quite a large company, which had gathered to make the acquaintance of the new judge of the circuit, the whole assemblage began at once to speak commiseratingly of the poor fellow, his lonely, friendless life, his lack of prospects, the weighty nature of his responsibilities.

"Why don't some one give him work?" asked the judge, who was a resident of a different county.

"Well—he—he isn't very strong—he can't do much—he came very near dying a short time ago," some one answered, and the judge replied "Oh!" in a tone which indicated that he completely understood the matter, and regarded it in the same light in which the citizens did. Lem passed the Squire's pastor one day in the street, and had in his face an expression which caused the good pastor to go instantly home and pray earnestly that the steps of this poor man might be ordered of the Lord. Lem happened in at the Methodist prayer-meeting one night, and noiselessly contracted himself into one of the rearmost corners; the next brother who prayed made a special appeal to heaven for Lem, mentioning the would-be beneficiary by name.

Lem grew steadily poorer, weaker and more anxious looking. When his money gave out he left his boarding-house and slept in a corn-rick; no one made remarks about it, for no one knew of it. Then he caught fish until the weather grew too cold for fishing, and the money for which he sold his fish paid for his lodging and board with a shiftless family living near the river. Whenever there was a freshet he sat in a skiff and watched the river for saw-logs; such of these as he secured gained him money enough to retain his miserable home. He cut wood on ground which a farmer wanted cleared, but he could do only about half the work of an able-bodied man, and there were many rainy days in which he could not work at all, so he never was able to spare money for his mother. Beggars, who occasionally visited Mount Zion and told pitiful stories, fared better than he, for Lem did not know how to beg.

He was not, with his many troubles, as badly off as he might have been, however, for he had three friends. The first was the old woman who had knit him a pair of socks when he was sick; the second was a little boy named Billy Miles; and the third, from whom he had once been estranged, but in whom he now found his only way into occasional oblivion, was whisky. The old woman, who lived by herself with barely enough to live upon, never had to cut her own fire-wood after Lem's recovery, as in previous days the villagers had allowed her to do. The little boy's heart Lem had won by teaching him to make spring-traps for birds, and the grateful little fellow had tried to repay Lem by teaching him Sunday school hymns and giving him a glass marble. The friendly service of whisky Lem could gain only by an outlay of money, but the expense was small as compared with the receipts.

But there were times when the companionship of neither of these friends sufficed—times when the thought of all he should do but could not do, drove him nearly to madness. People who were out of doors at night, occasionally met a spare, bent figure, who, when it thought itself unobserved, would make strange gestures and give forth strange, inarticulate sounds. If the moon were shining, they would see a face almost frightful in its eagerness. From behind the fringe of faces which surrounded the departing congregations on Sunday, the same countenance was often seen, until some of the more fastidious worshipers were heard to wish that

that dreadful looking fellow would leave the town. He haunted the doorways of churches, school-houses and the court-house, whenever any entertainment was given at either of them, and scrutinized the ground closely, as if hoping to see some one drop loose change near the door. At one time he gathered pecan-nuts, which had some commercial value, and sold them until he amassed several dollars, all of which money he parted with for the sake of consulting a fortune-teller, but without receiving any tangible return.

CHAPTER XIV.

A NEW EXPERIENCE.

As Lem crept about the streets one cold, dark night, looking downward and straight ahead as is the habit with the weaker beasts of prey, he suddenly heard, in spite of closed doors and windows, a mighty shout of song go up from the little Methodist church, where one of the daily evening services of a series known as " protracted meetings " was going on. There was something so assertive about the music—all vocal—that Lem unconsciously stopped and listened, and as the refrain again burst forth he caught the words:

O we'll land on the shore, O, we'll land on the shore, O we'll land on the shore, And we'll shout forevermore.

Such a rousing chorus Lem had never heard before. He approached the door, peered through the key-hole, lifted the latch as noiselessly as possible, and slipped into a back seat.

The scene Lem beheld speedily caused him to forget his troubles. The small, plain room, well lit by tallow candles, was full of men and women, mostly members of the church. The sermon had ended, and in response to an exhortation, several persons had knelt at wooden benches inside the altar-rail. Some of these were crying, and over all of them bent various members of the church, praying, instructing, and exhorting. Among the remaining members hymns and prayers had followed each other in rapid succession, a short and earnest exhortation from the pastor occasionally varying the order of exercises. At each response to the pastor's invitation to mourners to come forward, the enthusiasm of the congregation had increased, the prayers had become more fervid and the songs more spirited.

Lem looked about him in amazement. Could these really be the quiet, hard-working, rather depressed people he met about town every day? There was one man standing in the aisle with the face and air of a martial leader;—could that really be Asa Ringfelter, who usually shuffled about with apparently only the single idea of dodging Squire Barkum, to whom he owed more money than he could pay? And there, on the altar-steps, stood a man who had on a suit of clothes which Lem had last seen on his late host, Ben Ringsell; but the face—surely that supremely happy expression could not be developed from the doleful features which Ben had sufficient excuse to habitually carry. In an "amen" seat sat an old half-breed, who was undoubtedly the person always known at Mount Zion as "old Daddy Perks," and who had all the stolidity of his Indian parent; yet now he was crying with joy and shouting "Glory to God!" in tones heard easily above the loudest bursts of song. Old Aunty Bates Lem had always believed was an angel; but now, in spite of her wrinkles and straggling hairs and unutterably hideous bonnet, she *looked* like one. What could it all mean?

Every one but the few unbelievers knelt when the pastor called on Brother Brown to pray, and as the prayer, rugged in its structure but almost terrible in its earnestness, proceeded, the unbelievers themselves looked solemn; one of them attempted to create a diversion by throwing a cockle-burr upon the bald pate of a kneeling person, but the smiles excited were few and sickly.

When the prayer ended, good farmer Hake raised the following hymn, preceded by its chorus:

Sing his praise, ye lofty mountains; rolling oceans, mighty fountains;

roaring thunders, lightnings' blazes, Shout the great Redeemer's praises.

CHORUS.

Je - sus reigns: he reigns vic - to - ri - ous,

O - ver earth and heaven most glorious, Je - sus reigns.

The farmer, who had a soul full of poetry, although the only poems he ever read were in the hymn-book, led this first verse with a perfection of dramatic perfection never seen on the operatic stage; but he changed his tone as he led the next verse:

> Come ye sons of wrath and ruin,
> Who have wrought your own undoin'—
> Rebel sinners, royal favor,
> Now is offered by the Saviour.
>   Jesus reigns, etc.

At the close of this verse a tin-shop apprentice, with

9

a desperate but unsuccessful attempt to appear unaffect-
ed, hurried forward to the altar, and dropped at the
bench with a groan. Immediately the pastor ordered
another prayer, but Lem paid little attention to it; he
stared at the seat the apprentice had left, and wondered
why the young man, who was one of the principal evening lights of Micham's groggery, had gone to the altar.
His reflections were interrupted by Brother Benkess
starting the only hymn whose air he thought he knew,
but about which he was lamentably mistaken; this musi-
cal failure was brought to an early end by Father Dilman, who sang—

Hal - le - lu - jah, Halle - lu - jah, When my
last trial's o - ver, Hal - le - lu - jah; I
hope to shout glory, When the world's on fire, Hal-le - lu - jah.

This was followed by several verses of the old hymn
beginning—

" Jesus my all to heaven has gone,"

with the second and fourth lines of the above chorus appearing between the lines of the hymn. As Father Dilman, who had once been a sailor, proceeded with the hymn, he unconsciously found his way into the aisle, and strode up and down, shouting the words in staccato, with tremendous emphasis, and looking at every one enquiringly, as if to ask if they were not going to assist him at shouting in the new world; so at least the old man's face seemed to say to Lem, and the poor boy's heart gave a bound at the thought. The world on fire?—the last trial over?—oh, if it only were! and he and his father, and mother, and brothers, and sisters, could stand around the great white throne he had heard of, and shout with joy over the end of all sorrow and trouble!

Suddenly the whole tone of the meeting was changed by some one who started the refrain :

Re - mem - ber me, re-mem-ber me! O, Lord, re - mem - ber me!
Re - mem - ber Lord, Thy dying groans, And then re-mem - ber me !

Numerous verses from different hymns were sung to the same music, the refrain following each verse. The first few notes sobered the congregation, and made Lem

shiver; as the song continued, each successive couplet
sounded more and more like a beseeching wail; not a
single false note marred the inexorableness of the har-
mony, and the couplets seemed finally to change to blows,
each one more terrible than the last.   Lem trembled—he
grew pale—he grasped the rail of the seat before him,
lest he should fall.   His only comfort was that he was so
insignificant and uninteresting that no one would notice
him.   But he was mistaken; Aunty Bates turned her
head as some disturbance took place at the door, and saw
Lem, and something in his appearance caused her to put
on her spectacles and scrutinize him intently.   The instant the hymn was ended her cracked voice was heard
starting the hymn:

"Jesus, lover of my soul,"

to the air generally known as "Pleyel's Hymn."   The
audience was in exactly the right humor to render this
prayer—as both in words and music it was—in the right
spirit.   At the end of the first verse Lem broke down;
the words:

"Hide me, Oh, my Savior, hide,
Till the storm of life is passed,"

brought tears to his eyes, and though he dropped his

head upon the back of the seat in front of him, he could not conceal his emotion. Father Dilman, who had not recovered · from his excitement, noticed that Lem was greatly disturbed in mind, so he seated himself beside him, and said:

"Poor sinner, why don't you take up your cross and go forward for the prayers of God's people? *There's* the ark of safety—right up at that mourner's bench."

Lem still trembled and cried.

"Come right along," urged Father Dilman, laying an enormous hand on the weeping boy's shoulder. "There's always room for one more on the good ship Zion. There's a haven of rest for them that believe."

Lem only wept harder.

"Powerful convictions make glorious conversions," continued the old sailor, "an' you seem to have as much conviction aboard as a craft of your size can carry. Come along—I'll give you a tow if you think you can't make the mourners' bench under your own canvass. It'll make you feel better the minute you weigh anchor."

"I don't want to feel better," said Lem, half-choked apparently by his feelings. "I'm as happy as I *can* be

and live; I don't want *anything* but to die, and get out
of this awful world, and up to where God is."

The people were still wailing their way through
Wesley and Pleyel, but Father Dilman sprang upon a
seat and shouted:

"Another soul made port—Glory to God!" and then
the old sailor, with a voice against which the assembled
multitude strove only to submit, roared out:

I want to go, I want, to go I want to go
to hea - ven, I want to go where Je - sus is,
and have my sins for - giv - en. I'll tell you why I want to go;
I'll tell the pleas - ing sto - ry; There's so much troub -
le here be - low, but, oh, there's none in glo - ry.

Several of the brethren looked around inquiringly, and

finally made their way through the aisle to where Lem sat; they shook his hand, they congratulated him, and when the pastor, at the close of the meeting gave an opportunity to those who wished to unite with the church on probation, and Lem started forward to give the pastor his hand, the little knot of sympathizers led the audience in the doxology, beginning—

"Praise God from whom all blessings flow."

CHAPTER XV.

THE SQUIRE'S RELIGIOUS INTEREST IN LEM IS CRUELLY
ABUSED.

As LEM slowly awoke on the next morning, he gradually lost his desire to die and be among the angels. As he opened his eyes the least bit, and beheld the unattractive surroundings of his miserable apartment, he tried to conjure up the visions and sounds of the night before— the lights, the songs, the melodies, the transformed faces of men who usually seemed but little less troubled than himself—but without avail. Bare, cobwebbed rafters were what he saw; the rattling of culinary utensils, and the querulous voice of his landlady scolding her impudent children, were the sounds that he heard. He groaned, and buried his face in the straw of his ragged pillow, but a shout of " O, Lem!" roused him to see his landlord, a low-browed, blear-eyed, bestial man, standing at the head of the ladder which led to Lem's chamber.

"The fish is fried," remarked the landlord; and Lem

arose and performed his toilet by putting on his hat. By the act of descending the ladder, he came again into his old world —and the new, in spite of a frantic mental grasp, and eager stare and a great gulp in his throat, faded from his sight. He did not lose hope of recovering it, however. He despatched his breakfast with unusual celerity, and strolled up to the busier street of the town. He passed Micham's grocery, its doors surrounded by many of his old comrades, without much effort, but as he approached the principal stores he was tempted to run, and never show himself in town again. He longed to be spoken to by some one of the religious merchants, several of whom had been participants (not active) in the meeting, but he dreaded to hear what they might have to say. As he passed one after another of them, receiving only a pleasant yet conservative "Good morning" and an inquisitive stare, his pale face flushed with mingled expectancy and disappointment. What if even Christian bonds had no thread of sympathy in them?—there would then be no common meeting-ground on which he might find that response for which his heart was longing, even though he could not name it.

But Lem was not to be doomed to utter disappoint-

ment.   Faithful among the faithless, Squire Barkum
spied Lem from the rear of the store, and although the
good merchant was busily engaged in rubbing molasses
settlings into the brown sugar, he dashed out the front
door and laid a hand on the shoulder of his ex-employe.

"My dear young friend," said the Squire, as Lem
instinctively took a defensive attitude by thrusting his
hands into the pockets of his pantaloons, "I am
rejoiced to hear that you have taken a most excellent
and praiseworthy step.   I could have wished that you
might have cast your lot among *us*, for I have an abid-
ing conviction that our faith is more consoling and
unassailable than any other, but there are nevertheless, a
great many excellent people among the Methodists.
There's Captain Dilman, now—I've sometimes thought
that he was mighty shaky in doctrine, but he always
settles his account every winter, and there ain't no hon-
ester man in the whole county to trade horses with.
An' there's Jonathan Bingham—Jonathan's slow pay,
but I always believed he meant to do what he said.
How *is* it with your soul, Lemuel?"

Lem dropped his eyes.   He was not apt at formulating
his feelings, and on this particular morning he had no

feelings sufficiently distinct to admit of direct description; so he contemplated a tuft of grass growing between the bricks of the pavement, and remained silent.

"Don't you feel Christ in you, the hope of glory?" asked the Squire, with tender solicitude.

Lem still remained silent.

"Don't the Sperit bear witness with your sperit that you are born of God?"

"I guess it's all right, Squire," said Lem, at length, "but I don't exactly understand what you mean."

"Ain't you born again?" asked the Squire. "Tell me what your experience has been."

"Well," said Lem, "I went into the Methodist meetin'-house last night, an' everybody was happy, an' I found I was growin' happy too, an' I just let myself do it. I never seemed to see God an' feel him before, but last night I was sure I did. I felt as if I was ready to die an' go to him right away. But I don't feel that way now."

"That's nothin' wonderful," said the Squire, reassuringly. "Everybody's had the same experience. But don't let go your hope."

"I don't mean to," said Lem; "it's all I've got in the world."

The Squire darted a suspicious look at Lem. "I'm afeard, Lemuel," said he, "that the flesh is warrin' agin' the Sperit. Beware of that;—the carnal mind is at enmity against God."

"I don't know what the carnal mind is," said Lem; "but now that it's mornin', an' there's nothin' around to keep my mind on the strain it was last night, I get to thinkin' over the old trouble again—how I'm to do for mother——"

The Squire interrupted: "He that loveth father or mother more than me is not worthy of me—that's what Christ said, Lemuel."

"Well," said Lem, "if I got the right notion about him last night, he ain't a goin' to give me the go-by because I want to be a lovin' son and brother. This here's an awful world, Squire."

"It's only a sojournin' place, Lemuel," said the good old man; "heaven's the only home. Lay up your treasure in heaven, for where the treasure is there will the heart be also."

"'Tain't treasures that's botherin' me," said Lem; "it's the want of 'em—it's care."

"Cast all your care on him, for he careth for us," said the Squire.

"Is that in the Bible?" asked Lem.

"Yes, indeed, it is," said the Squire, hurrying into the back room of the store and bringing out one of the Bible Society volumes; "it's there, an' lots of other precious promises. Take this book, Lemuel—'twon't cost you anything—and may its precious truths be your daily meat an' drink."

Lem took the Bible with the air of a man who felt that other meat and drink he was not likely to find much of.

"Sit down, Lemuel," said the Squire, pointing to the chair. "You're a new traveler in the strait an' narrow way, but I've been in it a long time. I want to give testimony to the goodness of Almighty God. I've been on the road to Zion for nigh on to fifty year. I've had my share of the sorrows an' afflictions of life, but there never was a time when I needed strength that it wasn't give to me from above. As the psalmist says, there's been times when I'd have fainted if I hadn't seen the goodness of God, but I never was allowed to faint. An' you'll find it so too. Don't ever let yourself be cast down. The good book says, if any man lack wisdom, let him ask of the Lord, who giveth liberally, but let

him ask in faith, nothin' waverin'. An' if you don't
seem to get your mind clear, then come to me, an' profit
by the experience of an older hand at the business. I'm
your friend, Lemuel—I've showed it to you before in
earthly things, an' now I want to be your friend in
heavenly things. If I could help you any way, I'd feel
happy in it, knowin' I'd be doin' the will of my Father
in heaven. Oh, Lemuel, the ways of Providence are
mysterious an' past findin' out—who'd have supposed
that losin' your health when you started with Sam
Reeves' hoss-gang, would have brought you back to
where you was to find your Lord? An' to think that I,
that never expected any reward exceptin' in the approvin'
smiles of my heavenly Father, should have seen you
brought to him right here in the town that was the
scene of my labors for you. My dear boy,"—here the
Squire sprang to his feet and seized Lem's hand—

> "I give you here my heart an' hand,
> To meet you in the promised land."

Tears—honest tears—came into the Squire's eyes as he
said these last words, and pressed Lem's hand, while
poor, friendless, despondent Lem gave vent to his own
feelings after the manner which the Squire's example had

afforded. The world again seemed less the old scene of
sorrow and disappointment. The Squire's tears continued to flow, his rugged face softened into kindliness, and
he still held Lem's hand tightly in his own. The boy
looked at him wistfully, enquiringly, hopefully; he over-
came some obstruction in his throat, and at last stam-
mered out:

"I'm much obliged to you, Squire, I really am, more
than I can tell. I'm going to try to do everything that
the Bible tells me, an' that Christians tell me, an' I'll
take you up at your offer whenever I want advice. I
could be the best man in the world if it wasn't for—for
—oh, Squire, if you would only give me work—steady
work—so I wouldn't all the time be full of torment
about mother!"

The Squire's face froze at once into its accustomed
lines; his tears disappeared; he dropped Lem's hand and
said:

"That's out of the question, Lemuel; you know you
can't do my work, an' I can't keep two men. It'll all
come right—'seek first the kingdom of God an' His
righteousness, an' all these things shall be added unto
you.' I ain't got time to talk any more now, for here

comes the widow Meer with a crock of butter, an' it takes her a long time to trade. Commit thy way unto the Lord, an' he shall bring it to——butter, Mrs. Meer? —let's look at it; there's so much butter comin' in just now that we don't care to trade for any that ain't first class."

CHAPTER XVI.

THE HERO FORMS SOME MONEYED ACQUAINTANCES.

Lem hurried through the village toward the forest, in which the main street seemed to end. He walked so fast that the boys at the blacksmith shop stopped work to stare, and approaching countrymen looked enquiringly, and unconsciously slackened the pace of their slow-walking horses, as if they expected some news. Arrived at last at the edge of the woods, he threw himself on the doorstep of an abandoned toll-gate house, and groaned. For a few moments he breathed short and quick, as exhausted people always do, and then he began to murmur to himself:

"I wish to God I could die. I wonder if it *is* wrong for a feller to kill himself? If I was dead mother and the chidren wouldn't ever have any disappointment on my account any more. I wish I didn't ever have to see anybody in Mount Zion again; everybody looks at me this morning as if I was a menagerie. *Can't* somebody

10

ever even think to say a kind word, or even *look* kind, I
wonder, to a poor feller that never asks anything else of
'em but what he's willin' to work for?" The Squire—he
is just what everybody says—I swear he is; I wish I'd
have died before I met him this mornin'; nothin' ever
made the world look so awful before."

Inside the building, and but a few feet from Lem, two
men had listened to what he had said, and were now carrying on an animated conversation with every feature
except their lips. One of them, who looked like a weazel
not greatly overgrown, shook his head vigorously in
favor of some argument which his eyes had advanced;
the other, large, dark, sinister, and heavily bearded,
seemed in a receptive mood, but not convinced. Lem
continued:

"An' all this time there's mother a-waitin' an a-hopin'
an' a-listenin' for the mail-carrier, an' a-goin' to the post
office an' a comin' away without any letter, an' a-won-
derin' whether I'm dead; an' here's me, that hain't got
the grit to tell her I hain't got any money to send her.
Great God! Ain't it bad enough to be a good-for-nothin'
rack of bones that's no comfort to myself, without havin'
to be in this hell about money?"

Again the weazel-faced man inside snapped his eyes and set his teeth and shook his head furiously, and his companion yielded so far as to raise his eyebrows a trifle and look a little less sullen.

"Talk about sellin' a man's soul for money," Lem went on; "I'd sell *mine*—I'd sell it to the devil, if he wanted it, an' do it cheap. No body else seems to want it—p'raps them that's got money got it the same way. That old picture in the Sunday-Scoool book about the devil holdin' a bag of gold, an' ev'ry body runnin' after it —just wouldn't I like to be in that crowd? I wish he'd come along here this minute."

The smile which the weazel-faced man cast upon his companion, as he vigorously thrust forth a finger at him, indicated sufficiently that the devil was closer than Lem supposed; while the glare of satisfaction which came into the large man's eyes, would have impressed a beholder with the demonological idea that Satan was of divided or distributed personality. The small man softly arose and left the building, followed by his companion; the small man took from his pocket a roll of bills, and selected one of the denomination of twenty dollars, which he held up for the inspection of the other man, and received a nod

in acknowledgment.   Then they both made a short
detour in the woods, and reached a point in the road not
far from the gate-house.   Here the tall man laid down
by the road-side, while the smaller man, assuming an air
of great agitation, hurried on to the house and addressed
Lem:

"Stranger," said he, "do you want to make ten dollars?"

Lem sprang to his feet in an instant.

"Go right to town and buy me a dollar bottle of arnica
liniment; my mate's got a mighty bad sprain, an' can't
get up off the leaves till something's done for him.
Here's money to pay for it with—a twenty-dollar bill—
it's the smallest I've got—be sure you don't get any bad
bills in change."

"Don't—don't you want a buggy to get him into town
with?" asked Lem.

"No!" exclaimed the weazel-faced man, drawing near
to Lem, and whispering, "we're tracking a horse-thief,
and if he's in town he'd know us if we went in by daylight.   Not a word about us to anybody.   If you
shouldn't find me here when you come back, hang around
the house here till I come for you.   These are ticklish

times—we're afraid to let honest-looking farmers see us, even, for fear that they're in with horse-thieves. Now travel."

Lem started at a lively pace, but suddenly stopped and turned back.

"Is Bill Hixton the hoss-thief you're after?" said he.

"No," said the weazel-faced man, grown suspicious in an instant, "Bill Hixton's in jail in the next county. What do *you* know about him?"

"I know he's a horse-thief," said Lem, "but I know he saved my life once, an' that instid of buyin' you medicine I'd break your partner's legs, an' yourn too, to keep you from catchin' him if he was out."

The weazel-faced man grinned with delight. "Stick to your friends," said he, "that's the way I *like* to see a man do. Now hurry up, will you?"

Away went Lem, looking a year younger for every dollar of his prospective fee, while the weazel-faced man rejoined his companion.

"He's just the fellow we need," said he. "He's as green as grass, an' looks as if he could be trusted—tain't easy to find men you can trust in shoving counterfeits, either."

"Can't trust *him* after he finds out what business we're in," growled the large man.

"Now look here, Lodge, what's the use of gettin' down in the mouth that way, just when we've got a new man? S'pose he *does* only stick to us a few days; we've got the best-made money we ever had yet, and one way and another we'll manage to have him get off an average of a hundred a day. Countin' cost—sixteen and two-thirds per cent.—and makin' plenty of 'lowance for the trash we may have to buy that we don't want and can't sell, and for what we have to pay him, we ought to clear about seventy-five dollars a day. That's better than we ever done when we was in the nigger business."

The argument seemed unanswerable, for Mr. Lodge opened his mouth only to locate a piece of tobacco.

"That ain't all, either," argued he of the weazel face. "I believe we can tie that fellow to us so he'll never leave, even if he finds out everything," and the little man repeated Lem's remark about Bill Hixton, concluding as follows:

"Now, what I say is, let's pump him about his mother—you remember how he talked?—and give him fifty to send her."

"Fifty queer?" asked Mr. Lodge.

"No, fifty straight," said the little man. "It's a square business transaction, that's bound to hold together, and it's no place for foolin'. There's no knowin' what tight scrapes such a fellow mightn't get us out of."

Mr. Lodge pondered moodily over the proposed business risk, but suddenly his gloomy face grew radiant, and a commotion was visible under the thicket which covered his mouth and chin, as he remarked:

"Bill Hixton would give us five hundred—half of it down—if we'd help him break out. If you've got the story straight, this chap might be put up—not so's he'd know it—to take the risk and do the work. Then we'd clear four hundred and fifty. How's that, Binkle?"

The little man danced with ecstacy; not even a blackberry cane that attached itself to his coat and yearningly reached the cuticle upon Mr. Binkle's shoulder, succeeded in subduing his ecstacy. He even gave vent to several short shrieks of delight, which were discontinued only after the more sedate Mr. Lodge had made an earnest appeal, in language almost wholly scriptural, for silence.

"We'll take the ten you was going to give him out

of the fifty he's to send his mother," suggested Lodge, but the business-like Binkle replied:

"No, we won't. He'll want to spend something for himself, maybe, and he ought to spend *some* good money, in case anybody should get on the scent. I believe he's coming now—yes, it must be—*somebody's* coming, with a bottle in his hand. Thunder! I didn't make up a yarn for him to tell about what he wanted the liniment for."

"Just like you, always goin' off half cocked," growled the little man's partner, who had sunk already into his habitual despondency. "Let's get up into the timber, an' keep an eye on the fields—some infernal constable may be trackin' him."

Both men climbed trees near the edge of the woods, and scrutinized the ground between them and the town. As wheat stubble was all that the fields contained, they soon satisfied themselves that Lem was not followed. Then they descended, and when Lem arrived, panting and purple, Mr. Binkle welcomed him with a look of tender solicitude, and led him to a thicket a hundred yards from the road, where lay Mr. Lodge caressing a bandaged ankle, and simulating pain with heart-rending groans.

CHAPTER XVII.

A MISDIRECTED MISSIONARY EFFORT.

For several days Lem's new friends kept him quite
busy. They assured him of steady employment, explain-
ing that officers of the law, who, like themselves, could
not be too careful to keep their own persons out of sight,
needed some assistant who was well known and trusted.
The work made necessary by the pursuit of the horse-
thief for whom they were ostensibly in search, was
various. Among other things, a gun was necessary—
they had forgotten to bring their fire-arms, so great had
been their hurry—and Lem was sent to the principal
settlement in the adjoining county to buy one, the cost
not to exceed ten dollars, though a fifty dollar bill was
given him with which to make the purchase. Then
Lem was instructed to hire a horse, on pretense of going
to see a cousin in still another county, and there he was
to purchase, out and out, three as good horses as he
could find. These investments were made only after

Lem had been sent into Mount Zion on every conceivable errand by which good money could be obtained in exchange for counterfeits. Mr. Binkle had fulfilled his intention of giving Lem fifty dollars for his mother, the giving having been preceded by a drawing from Lem of his story, and by a copious shower of tears from the sympathetic Mr. Binkle.

As for Lem, he was happy; life seemed every way delicious to him. He was helping his mother; he was satisfying his employers; he had at last found some one who appreciated him and remunerated him handsomely. There was something delightful about the secrecy of his new business, and even more delightful in the camping out and the irregular life which it necessitated. Money came to him freely; he was promised a regular salary of twenty-five dollars per month, but before he had been among the counterfeiters a week, he had received, in good money, and as special gratuities for successful transactions, the equivalent of his monthly salary. The conservative Mr. Lodge murmured considerably about his partner's generosity, and finally remarked:

"You might pay it in bad money, anyhow — *he* wouldn't know any better."

"Them storekeepers down East, where his mother'll spend whatever we give him, would spot it in a minute," replied Mr. Binkle, "and then we *might* lose *him.* You muscn't forget the first principles of business, Lodge, just for the sake of being careful."

"'Spose we lose him anyhow?" growled the despondent partner.

"*Then* we'll have got rid of a good deal more than we ever did in such a little while before. You don't even seem to think that we're doin' good with money we give him, either."

Mr. Lodge uttered a frightful bark, which was intended for sarcastic laughter; his partner so understood it, for he took issue with him at once.

"Now look here, Lodge, 'tisn't decent in you to always talk and act as if we were the hardest cases in the world. You may think what you please about yourself, but when you're thinkin' up abuse, just count me out, if you please. I know shovin' counterfeit money isn't accordin' to law, but I hain't got the same notions on finance that congressmen and legislators have, and when I get a chance to do good, and it don't cost more than I think I can stand, I'm going to do it, and I ain't ashamed to say that I believe it'll be passed to my credit. Over and over again I've heard preachers get off sermons on the text, 'True religion and undefiled is this: to visit the fatherless and the widows in their affliction, and to keep themselves unspotted from the world.' I'm doin' the *fust* half of that by givin' Lem plenty of money to send to his mother. The *last* half of the text — well, there's lots of church members in business that's worse than me. I don't drink, I don't swear, I don't steal, I never tell dirty stories, no woman alive can say anything against me—"

"How about the mother of that boy that the Regulators hung in Missouri, for shovin' bad money that you gave him to spend?" interrupted Mr. Lodge.

"I didn't mean *that* sort of thing about women," replied Mr. Binkle, quickly, "and you ain't fair in throwin' it up to me—you know I'd have got him the best lawyer in the country, and got him clear, when the case came for trial, or I'd have hired somebody to break jail for him; I thought a great deal of that boy. You can throw up such things against me all you've a mind to— *I* don't care—once in grace, always in grace, and I know I once was there. What bothers me is that *you* don't pay any attention to such things. I don't like to pester you about 'em, because it always makes you so glum, but I *do* feel as if it was my duty sometimes. You'd feel a good deal happier if you were to have a hope of something better in another world, and you wouldn't be so awfully scared every time you thought anybody was on your track. A man don't have to be a saint because he's a Christian—everybody's imperfect, but if they trust in the merits of Christ——"

"O, shut up, will you?" growled the impenitent counterfeiter.

"No, I won't," said Mr. Binkle. "I stand everything you say to me, and you don't always mean it for my good, either; what I'm saying to you is all in dead earnest and good feeling, and there's no money in it for *me.* You don't 'spose I'm enjoyin' it, talking to such a determined reprobate as you are, do you? I'm doin' it because it's for your good, an' because it's my duty."

"You're a model preacher, *you* are," retorted Mr. Lodge, darker-faced and heavier-browed than ever. " You had a good bringin' up, I reckon, from what you let drop; you might have made a decent livin' anywhere, but you took to counterfeit money. *I* was only a loafer—a cross between half-breed and white trash, and I never hurt anybody but myself, except when I got too much whisky in me and went into a fight, and *then* I never gave any worse than I took. You paid a fine for me, and got me out of jail, and then learned me *this* infernal business; I wish you'd left me in jail; I never felt so bad there as I've done ever since I've been with you, and got in with hoss-thieves and all sorts of rascals, such as a decent drinkin'-shop wouldn't let come in doors. Whenever there's been any ugly work to do— puttin' a bullet into a sheriff, or stealin' horses to get out of the country with—I've had to do it. You've spoiled lots of other fellers in the same way; you've made likely young farmers turn rascals; you've filled poor people's pockets with money that some day or other they find out is counterfeit; you've spiled boys that might have made decent men if you'd let 'em alone— you don't ever go anywhere but somebody's got to be in risk of his neck. And then to talk religion to me! What do you think about your own string?—ain't it long enough to take up your whole time?"

Mr. Binkle had winced repeatedly under his companion's attack, but toward the end he somewhat recovered himself. He looked thoughtfully, almost sentimentally, into the sky, and finally sighed out:

"I'm a miserable sinner, I know."

"Glad to hear you own up," growled Lodge.

"Everybody's a sinner," continued Mr. Binkle, "and I'm not going to try to sneak out of my share. After all said and done, my iniquities rise like a mountain."

"That's somethin' like," said Mr. Lodge.

"My debt to divine justice is such as I can never begin to repay ——"

"Pile it on—don't be afraid of making it too thick," interrupted Mr. Lodge.

"But," continued Mr. Binkle, his voice falling a little, and his words coming a little slower, "there's *one* comfort; however great the debt is, Jesus paid it all."

The sentiment to which Mr. Binkle gave voice, is one which has released countless men and women from bondage to their own fears; it has been for two thousand years the last hope, and at times the only encouragement, of souls full of honest aspirations, yet painfully conscious of the drawbacks caused by their own imperfections; it has raised millions upon millions into a clearer comprehension of the possible greatness of love, and of love's legitimate end, than unaided nature could ever have given them; it has inspired the greatest works of the greatest artists; it has melted the savage, strengthened the saint, persuaded the sinner; it has been the motive power of civilization's mightiest advances during ages in which imperfect humanity could not so easily comprehend the lesson of Christ's life as that of his death. But, reduced to a mere cold, commercial condition, as in the mind of Mr. Binkle and many another utterly selfish man of business it actually is, no one can wonder that it does not take possession of irreligious persons who fall under the influence of such men, and that it appears to them what to millions of mean natures it actually is—a substitute for conscience, and a convenient mask to conceal from a man the actual lineaments of his own rascalities. And so it came to pass that Mr. Lodge, instead of being religiously affected by the speech of his companion, bent upon that gentleman a look in which scorn, curiosity and admiration were so strangely blended, that any painter who could have caught Mr. Lodge's expression, might have gained fame and fortune for himself.

CHAPTER XVIII.

THE WISDOM OF SERPENTS.

" Did you see him?"

" I reckon."

" Is he up to business?"

" O, isn't he!"

" When?"

" Right off."

" Square?"

" Here's the two-fifty advance."

The speakers were Messrs. Binkle and Lodge, the latter acting as interrogator. As Mr. Binkle made the final reply recorded above, he drew from his pocket a roll of bank-notes, which Bill Hixton had paid him in advance for the still-to-be-performed service of securing his escape from jail. Mr. Lodge examined the notes closely, and finally remarked:

" They all seem to be good."

" Of course they're good," replied Mr. Binkle, " you

11

never heard of Bill Hixton playin' a trick in a business transaction, did you?"

Mr. Lodge did not deign to reply, but said, instead:
"Lets put the boy up to it, right away."

"Just the way we agreed on?" asked Binkle.

"I 'spose there's nothin' better," said the non-committal Lodge.

"Here he comes now," said Mr. Binkle, "not too quick, now."

Lem appeared from the direction of the town, where he had been to forward to his mother his latest accumulations. As was his custom, he seated himself at some distance from his employers, to give them an opportunity to discuss their (supposed) professional duties.

"Come along, Lem — no secrets here to-night," shouted Mr. Binkle. Lem accepted the invitation, and stretched himself upon the ground, near the bed of hot coals which the financial operators had cherished. Mr. Binkle was staring into the fire with a most virtuous expression of countenance, while his partner was nursing the bandaged ankle. Both counterfeiters were silent for some moments; then Mr. Binkle groaned, and remarked:

"It's an infernal shame."

"That's so," responded his partner.

"Bill Hixton would make a splendid man; he's got in him the stuff for a lawyer, or even a preacher, if he would just stick to decent ways, and stop making trouble for us—officers of the law."

"What's he up to?" asked Lem, recognizing the name, and showing himself full of interest at once.

"Oh, nothing," said Mr. Binkle. "But I dropped into —— county jail to-day, to see if anybody else had caught the man we're lookin' for, an' there was Bill. It made me feel bad."

"What d'ye 'spose he'd go at if he got out?" asked Mr. Lodge.

"Well, I don't know," said Mr. Binkle, whipping his own pantaloons as he meditated. "I argued with him that he was makin' a fool of himself, stealin' hosses for a livin', when he was so fit to adorn society, and he owned up he was ashamed of himself."

"He's a good man," exclaimed Lem. "He done more for *me* than anybody else ever did, and he never saw me before, either."

"Well," said Mr. Binkle, with a resigned sigh, "*if* there's any good in him, he'll get a chance to show it out pretty soon—that's *my* opinion. His cell window is broader and deeper than he is, and it'll be the easiest thing in the world for somebody to pass him in a good flat file, like that one I took from a horse-thief and dropped under the toll-house the other day. If somebody was to give him such a file, and stand outside to help him when ·he tried to wriggle out, I believe Bill would be where nobody could find him in less than six hours."

"Like enough *then* he'd go right back to his old ways," said the desponding Mr. Lodge.

"Depends on who lets him out," said Mr. Binkle. "If it should be one of his old gang, he'd off an' steal a hoss within two hours; if it was a man that really cared for him, an' would give him a little moral lecture, he'd like as not break for some new country an' join the church."

"Well!" groaned Mr. Lodge, again squeezing his bandaged ankle, "I guess there ain't any chance for him. It's too bad, but he ain't the kind of feller that decent men takes a risk on, an' tain't the thing for officers of the law to think about as happenin' any way."

"I don't know 'bout that," said Mr. Binkle. "It's so

easily done that it's our business as officers to think it
over and scare up some new way of makin' prisoners
more secure in jail. Suppose, now, that Bill had a friend
at Mount Zion, or any other place as near to the jail that
he's in. It's about eleven miles; they could go quietly
along in the timber by daylight, hang around in the
edge of the town till midnight, get Tom out in two
hours, and be back home an' in bed 'fore daylight. That
ain't the way that jails ought to be—nobody watchin'
the roads, or anything."

"It's too bad, anyhow," said Mr. Lodge, "but it isn't
business. S'pose we go down the river road for a couple
of days an' see if we can't catch *our* man. It'll give
Lem a chance to rest, and he hasn't had one lately."

"It's a game," said Mr. Binkle. "Let's start at once."

Lem did his best to help his employers off. Two of
the new horses were saddled, and the third was led.
Lem assisted Mr. Lodge into the saddle, and the party
started. No sooner was it out of sight, than Lem was
under the toll-gate house, searching for the file of which
his respected partner had spoken. He heard a rustling
in the underbrush, and started out guiltily, but it was
only Mr. Binkle, who said:

"Meet us here, Lem, say on the morning after day after to-morrow—we may catch our man, and then you'd be useful. Get plenty of sleep between now and then if you can—it may come in handy."

Mr. Binkle rode away, and Lem plunged into the bushes beside the road to Friendlytown, where Hixton was confined.

CHAPTER XIX.

FRIENDS IN COUNCIL.

On a cool Autumn evening, Mr. William Hixton lay on the uninviting bed of the only cell in Friendlytown jail, and indulged in bitter reflections. He should have been asleep; other people slept. There was not even a streak of light visible under the door of any liquor-shop in the town. A volunteer orchestra of owls and other night-birds, assisted by a chorus of frogs, dogs and mosquitos, was emitting chords discordant enough to drive one to sleep in pure self-defense. But Mr. Hixton failed to sleep, from any cause whatever. He soliloquised and he swore; the latter operation is unworthy of repetition, but the results of the former conveyed a certain amount of information which the reader may possibly find available.

"Court'll sit—let's see—day after to-morrow, as sure as I'm alive, and there ain't a lawyer on the circuit that's smart enough to get me off, even if the Regulators don't snatch me out and string me up to a tree before that. If Binkle's little game works, all right; if it should hang fire, I'd be worse off than I am now. Darn it, it *would* be tough to string me up, if I *am* a—a dealer in hoss-flesh. Queer how things go in this world; I've never done anything but make off with a few horses, and yet I'm in jail, while there's Binkle, that's made a hundred times as much money in a way that ain't any better, has never been caught at it yet. There's something wrong in the way this world's managed. Hello! what's that?"

Mr. Hixton's soliloquy had been interrupted by a sharp, low whistle. The prisoner put under the cell window a stool, upon which he sprang, and stood on tip-toe.

"I don't know that whistle," said he, after scanning the jail-yard intently for some minutes. "Confound it, this world's so dishonest that nobody knows who to trust. Mebbe Binkle's sent some green man—mebbe, again, it's some of them infernal Regulators. If they come, I wonder how many there'll be of 'em? Them two revolvers that Binkle left me would clean out a common crowd —I don't believe anybody else in this God-forsaken country has got a revolver, or knows what one is. And my knife—oh, I guess I could get out, but then there'd be the job of hidin'. Dog-gone it, why *can't* they let business men alone?"

Again the horse-thief heard the whistle, and at the same moment there was a shadow at his cell window, and something fell with a sharp metallic ring upon the floor.

"A file, bless the Lord!" exclaimed the thief, groping on the floor with his hands. Suddenly a slight rustling and another metallic jingle was heard, and the file was snatched up to and out of the grating again. The horse-thief let slip a violent exclamation, and sprang upon his stool beneath the grating. At the same time another face appeared outside the grating. The two shadows confronted each other, and indulged in the following dialogue:

"You know what that was? 'Twas a file—you could cut your way out with that in an hour or two."

"I know it. Why the —— didn't you leave it there after you got it in?"

"'Cos I want to talk to you fust. If I help you get out, what are you goin' to do?"

"Goin' to do?—I'm goin' to get out of this neighborhood as soon as I can, and *stay* out of it."

"What are you goin' to do for a livin'? That's what I mean."

"Do what I always done, I s'pose."

"You musn't—it ain't right. There's folks—smart folks, that ought to know—that say you're good for something better."

"I wish they'd give me a chance at it, then."

"Will you use it if you get it?"

"Yes, I will."

"What'll you do?"

"Go to Texas and raise stock."

"Have you got any family?"

"Yes—I've got a——curse you, I believe you're an officer."

"No I ain't."

"You're tryin' the friendly dodge to get information out of me to use against me. You needn't come any of your infernal high moral tricks on me—I'm up to trap."

"You needn't be afraid of me. I'll stick tighter to you than any friend you've got, if you'll only not hurt me after you get out by goin' back to—to—"

"Hoss-stealin?"

"I 'spose that's the only name for it. Mebbe if I get you out *I'll* get caught, an' be sent to States prison. An' I'm willin.' Only—*have* you got any family?"

"I've got a mother, but you won't find out anything more until—"

"I don't want to find out anything more. But just think how happy you'd make *her*— a big, smart feller like you—if you'd only do what's right. There's fellers that's got mothers an' ain't fit to be any comfort to 'em, an' they just envy you, and wish they had your grit and headpiece. *They* don't take to hoss-stealin'—they hang around, starvin' and hopin, an' gettin' scared to death."

"Have *you* got a mother?"

"Yes."

"Then you shan't help *me* out. Go away. Tie the string with the file on it to the gratin'—I won't draw it in till you're safe out of sight."

"I won't do it—you mightn't get safe to the ground, and if you got lamed you might get catched."

"Go away, any how—I'd rather run my chance than get you in jail 'cause I got out. I don't mind tellin' you that somebody else is goin' to get me out if you don't.

I'm safe—go along, but you might leave the string where I can reach it."

" You won't go back to the old business, even if somebody else let's you out, will you?"

" No—I swear to God I won't."

There was a slight rustle of the garments of the shadow outside the grating; then a small black square shadow appeared beside the larger one outside; it was thrust through the grating, with the words—

" Kiss the book."

The sound of moving lips was heard.

" You might as well keep the book now you've got it," whispered the outer shadow. " I ain't an extra-good reader, an' there's things in it that I don't make out, but they say it's the best thing in the world for men that's tryin' to turn over a new leaf. Here's the file—remember your mother. I'll sneak up an' help you out when you're ready."

" Steady!" whispered the other shadow. " Give me your hand—count on me for life. Who are you?—how can I let you know where I get to, and how can you reach me if you ever need money or friends?"

"I'm the feller you gave a hoss to once, an' then saved him from the Regulators."

"Great God!" exclaimed the other shadow. Then it snatched the file and began work, with an energy not justly attributable to shadows.

At the same moment a figure glided away from the inner door of the cell, where it had been crouching during the entire conversation. It passed through the narrow hall-way which separated the cell from the jailor's apartments, noiselessly opened a door, slipped rapidly along the wall, and peered around the corner of the building in time to see Lem crouch behind a barrel near the fence. Then the figure withdrew its head, passed under cover of the jail to a street, went noiselessly and with bare feet through the street, down an alley, and into another alley, on one side of which was the high board fence of the jail.

The scene which here met his eye did not seem to surprise him, but it was nevertheless unusual and peculiar. Fifteen or twenty men—all of them respectable, hard-working citizens, and some of them church-members — were ranged along the fence, peering through cracks and knot-holes, and each man held a pistol of some sort.

The new-comer glided along the line, scrutinizing each man, and receiving friendly nods in return. At length he seemed to find the man for whom he was searching, and, laying his hand on his shoulder, exclaimed:

"Major, this thing's got to stop."

"Why, what in thunder's the matter, Sheriff," whispered the Major, straightening himself up, and pocketing his pistol, while two or three other men approached them and thrust their heads forward.

"I can't easily tell what's up," said the Sheriff. "I wish you'd all heard it for yourself. I've heard enough to make me Bill Hixton's friend. There ain't to be any lynching around here to-night. I'll stop his breakin' out, if you say so, but if I do you've got to agree not to break in."

"Can't you tell what the —— you're drivin' at?" demanded the man upon whose horse Lem was riding a few months before, when he was captured by the Regulators.

The Sheriff seemed to swallow something, not with the greatest success; then he spoke in a low, dogged tone:

"It's just this; that chap that's helpin' him is the

poor little cuss that Bill gave your hoss to, and that the
rest of the crowd came near hangin', only that Bill was
man enough to come in and tell the truth, and get some
cold lead for his pains."

"Then the little scoundrel *was* in with Bill and his
gang," said the Major. "That's just the way us fellows
let business slip through our fingers when we're excited."

"No, he wasn't," replied the Sheriff. "Bill didn't
know who he was to-night till the very last minute.
And the way that little cuss preached to him—why it
would have converted the devil, he was so infernally in
earnest about it."

"Bill Hixton's *worse* than the devil," whispered Garman. "Who ever caught the devil prowlin' around an'
stealin' honest farmers' hosses?"

"Well, Bill's a man of his word, any way," said the
sheriff, "an he gave that boy his word that if he got out
he'd give up the road, and go to Texas and raise stock.
And what do you think?—that little cuss was so sharp
that he stuck a Testament through the window, and
made Bill swear on it."

"If he comes to trial," said the Major, reflectively,
"he'll get the full term—twenty years. He'd *rather* be

hung by Regulators than stay in jail that long, if there's
any live spirit in him. And then if he ever did break
out, he'd be worse than ever—men always grow worse
in jail than they do anywhere else."

"Why not let him get out to-night?" said the Sheriff.
"I'm the one it'll come hardest on; I'll lose my re-
election by it, and p'raps get something worse. *You*
fellows haven't got anything to lose by it."

"I didn't lose a hoss by him, I s'pose?" growled Garman.

"You've got him back, and a decent saddle with him,"
retorted the Sheriff; "you may steal *my* horse every
week on those terms, if you like."

One by one the Regulators left their points of observa-
tion and clustered about the speakers, until only one
man remained watching the jail. Suddenly the watcher
cocked his pistol; in an instant the Sheriff snatched it
away. Looking through a knot-hole, he saw the prisoner's head and shoulders emerging from the window, while
Lem stood on a box beneath the window, trying to assist.

"Boys," said the Sheriff, rapidly and hoarsely, "let
him go. I swear here before the whole crowd to own
up to the whole trick myself, if Bill's ever heard of
again as being at his old tricks. I'll—"

"He's getting out," whispered a man on the look-out. "Duty! boys—duty!"

Fully half the men sprang toward the fence. The Sheriff snatched his pistols from his pocket, ran back and forth, pushing men back, as he whispered—almost hissed:

"There, I'll do *my* duty. By virtue of the authority in me vested by the State of Illinois, I command you to disperse, and allow me to re-capture my prisoner. These pistols are revolvers—six shots apiece. I'll shoot the first man who lays a hand on or fires a shot at my prisoner — so help me God!"

"Have it your own way, Sheriff, if you mean to re-capture," said the Major with exquisite blandness, after a moment, in which every one had dropped his pistol-hand. "You agree to call on us if you need help to grab him?"

"Yes," whispered the Sheriff, peering through a crack in the fence. "Here he comes—the little chap with him—they're talkin'—now listen for yourselves."

Everybody squeezed close to the fence. The horse-thief and his deliverer reached a corner of the fence and halted. Hixton faced Lem and put out his hand.

12

" You're the first real friend I ever had in my life," said the thief, " and I don't know how to thank you enough."

" You don't owe me anything," said Lem, " only don't get into the old business again. Remember your mother."

" I wish I had something to give you," said Hixton, but I gave all my money to a counterfeiter the other day, to have me got out; and the Sheriff seems to have found my revolvers and packed 'em out on the sly—I couldn't find 'em just now when I got ready to leave."

" I'll give you the money *I've* got—you can send it to my mother—Mrs. Pankett, Middle Backville, New York, when you earn it, honestly," said Lem.

" I won't take it," said Hixton. " I can work my way wherever I go. Look here, boy, you want to look out for yourself. There's hard cases in this part of the State just now, and you're the sort of a fellow they'll get for to do their dirty work for 'em. If you see any strangers with plenty of money, shy off from 'em,— you hear?"

" Never mind me," said Lem; " remember everything you've promised."

"If this thing should be tracked to you," said the thief, "I'll hear about it some way, and see that you're helped to break out."

"I don't want you to," said Lem. "'Twould get you in with your old crowd again. I'd rather be tried and go to the penitentiary than have you do that."

Outside the fence, Mr. Garman slipped up to the sheriff, and whispered:

"Let him go, Sheriff, for the boy's sake—*he's* clear grit."

"Good-bye, my boy—time's flyin', and I must have my tracks covered before daylight," said the thief.

Lem dropped on his knees and leaned against Hixton. "You're the best friend *I* ever had," said he. "I hope I'll see you g in some day."

The horse-thief stooped and put his hands on the boy's head. "I'll keep track of *you*," said he, "and if I don't behave myself for any other reason, I'll do it to oblige the only man who ever put himself out on my account. Now, travel—I won't get over this fence till I see you off—our roads don't run the same way."

Lem hurried off to the front of the yard; at the same time the Major approached the sheriff and whispered:

"Let him off for his *own* sake!"

The thief climbed the fence; the Sheriff still held his pistols, seeing which Mr. Garman quietly seized one arm and the Major the other. The thief reached the top of the fence, saw the crowd, and growled:

"Who the devil are *you?*"

"Friends," replied the Major, "who were going to lynch you half an hour ago. Get out!"

Mr. Hixton followed his instructions with praise-worthy alacrity.

CHAPTER XX.

IN WHICH THE HERO STICKS TO HIS FRIENDS.

WHEN Lem approached Mount Zion through the early dawn of the following morning, it was with aching head and weary limbs. Whatever qualms of conscience he had suffered during his long walk were lost in a mind never strong, and now too exhausted to consider questions of causistry. Reaching the abandoned toll-house, he dropped upon the floor, and was asleep in an instant.

How long he slept he did not know, but he was finally aroused by feeling hands in his pockets. Opening his eyes, he found the hands belonged to the Sheriff of his own county, while that officer's deputy sat upon the floor a few paces away. Lem started up and the Sheriff retreated a step or two, looking at the startled boy with an expression of the most sincere sorrow. '

" I'm awfully sorry for you, Lem," said the Sheriff; " sorrier than I ever was for anybody, except that splendid steamboat clerk that I had to hang for killing a man.

I never supposed you'd come down to running counterfeits on people."

"I haven't," said Lem, indignantly.

"I hope you didn't know about it," replied the Sheriff, "but it looks bad; there's four or five bills been traced back to you, and I've got a warrant for your arrest, and I searched you while you were asleep, thinking you mightn't feel so bad about it as if you were awake. You don't seem to have any bad money about you now. Suppose, now, you explain how you got the bills that you spent in town, and maybe you can clear yourself before the thing can be made public."

Lem looked vacant, then confused, then dogged and sullen. The Sheriff watched his face closely, and finally asked:

"You didn't know they were counterfeits, did you?"

"No," said Lem with such vehemence that, added to the look of outraged innocence his face took on, almost assured the officer that Lem was guiltless.

"Where did you get them, then?" asked the Sheriff.

Lem pondered a moment, and replied: "If I tell, *other* folks'll be arrested the same way, I s'pose. · I won't do it. Besides, they'll tell themselves when they find that I've got into trouble about it."

"I hope they will, any way," said the Sheriff, "but until the matter's cleared up, I'll have to hold you a prisoner."

"Will—will I have to go to jail?" asked Lem. The Sheriff nodded gravely, and the unhappy prisoner dropped his head. Though he drew his hat down over his eyes, the Sheriff soon saw tears trickling down Lem's face.

"I'll tell you what I'll do, Lem," said the Sheriff, "I'll leave you here, with Turner to watch you, until dark; then he can bring you up to the jail without anybody seeing you. And I'll not let on in town that we've found you, and I'll say everywhere that I don't believe you knew anything about the kind of money you were passing— I *don't* believe it, either."

"Thank you very much," said Lem; "and like enough it'll be all explained away before then."

"Well, Turner, you look out for him," said the Sheriff. "Have you got a deck of cards with you?"

"I reckon," said the deputy.

"Got pipes and tobacco?"

"Only one pipe."

"I'll lend Lem mine, then," said the Sheriff, producing

a clay bowl with a reed stem. "Lem, my boy, will you give me your word that you won't try to run? I'm doing what I can for *you*."

"Yes, I will, Sheriff," said Lem. "I'm not afraid of anything happening to *keep* me in jail, and I'd rather be cleared in town than run away an' dodge it."

"Hurrah for he!" said the Sheriff. "I guess you'll come out all right. Now I'll put. I've been hanging around here all night."

The afternoon wore away rapidly. Lem smoked more than his weak head could stand with comfort, and played old sledge very steadily, for whatever intervals of thought he had were not comforting in their results. He hoped Binkle and Lodge would return, and at once clear him, as they undoubtedly could. Once there came into his head, as quickly and painfully as he imagined a bullet might have done, Bill Hixton's parting remark about strangers with plenty of money. Could it be that his friends were not officers after all? Might they not be dealers in bad money? The thought was so terrible that he absent-mindedly played his knave upon his companion's queen, though he had two smaller trumps in his hand.

Suddenly, as both men had their heads together, trying to light fresh pipes with the same match, there was a shadow cast from the doorway toward which the deputy had his back; before the officer could look around to ascertain the cause, he received a tremendous blow on the head, which knocked him senseless, while Lem, looking up, beheld Bill Hixton.

"Get out that door and onto my horse—he's where your bosses used to tie theirs—and gallop down to New Philadelphia; there's a boat just leaving Mount Zion, and you'll catch it if you gallop lively. Here's money—plenty of it—don't stop till you reach Vicksburgh—I'll meet you there in a week or two."

"I won't do it," said Lem.

Mr. Hixton straightened himself from the stooping posture in which he had been blindfolding and tying the unconscious deputy, and stared fixedly at Lem. Recovering his tongue, he asked:

"Why not?"

"Because my bosses 'll clear me when they get back, an' I'm not goin' away with a bad name."

The ex-thief picked Lem up as if he had been a baby, carried him through the underbrush to where the horse was tied, saying as he walked:

"Your bosses, Binkle and Lodge, are the smartest shovers of counterfeit money in the whole West—they've been playing it on you this week or so. I met 'em not three hours ago, and heard all about it. They'd heard about the warrant out for you, and I believe they were both real sorry for you, but they're a couple of infernal cowards, and wouldn't try to rescue you. They talked about lettin' you go to jail, and then hiring somebody to break you out. I told 'em *I'd* 'tend to that job. Now gallop your liveliest, and do as I tell you to."

"I gave the Sheriff my word that I wouldn't run away," said Lem.

Hixton set Lem upon the horse, and drew a pistol.

"Mind me!" said he.

Lem looked at the pistol, and shuddered; then he asked:

"Where did you get this horse?"

"Bought him—I'm a man of my word, youngster."

"Where did you get the money?"

"Of Binkle."

"Counterfeit?"

"No—he owed me two hundred and fifty, good money, that I paid him to do what he *didn't* do; he was to have sent somebody to break me out of jail. He made believe he sent *you*, and told me how he put the notion in your head, but when I told him of the way that you and me had met twice before, he owned up beat, and shelled out the money. Now look here, my boy, you've saved my neck, but I once saved yours, and I demand a favor of you. Do as I tell you, and get out of this country. You can't do any good by stayin'—*if* you go, you can count on me for life, and see your folks well taken care of. If you *don't* go, I'll get on this horse, ride into town, give myself up to the Sheriff, and swear that *I* run that money on you!"

Lem gathered up the reins, Hixton pulled a twig from a tree and gave the horse a sharp cut, and away dashed the animal at a pace which compelled Lem to hold tightly to mane and saddle to keep from falling.

"Tie him in front of the warehouse at New Philadelphia," shouted Hixton; then he exclaimed in a deep undertone: "Thunder! that infernal deputy sheriff must have heard that—I'll have to put *him* where his boss can't find him."

CHAPTER XXI.

PUBLIC OPINION.

BAD news and damaging reports traveled as rapidly at Mount Zion as they ever did in the best society, so it came to pass that everybody soon knew the worst about Lem, and, apparently, a great deal in addition to the truth. The news was undoubtedly received with sincere regret by many good people, but these were of the kind who did not enjoy gossip. Many others seemed to find a kind of satisfaction in the import of the stories. A knot of men, who were waiting at the post-office for the arrival of the mail, listened to such reports as each other had heard, and when one of them expressed the opinion that Lem was a bad egg, he did not hear a dissenting voice.

"Like enough it was all a trick, his getting to Mount Zion the way he did," suggested Major Moydle, who was the most brilliant theorist and irresponsible purchaser in the county.

"What, and smash up a steamboat to do it?" asked the postmaster.

"Like enough," replied the Major, cocking his hat over his eye in a most defiant manner, and assuming an attitude of self-defense. "There's nothing that such fellows won't do to carry their point. The pilot of that boat said that the least turn of the wheel one way or the other, would settle everything in such a scrape as that was. He swears *he* didn't turn it—probably he didn't; but how easy it would have been for that Lem to have had a line fastened to one of the steering-chains near the rudder, and have given it a little bit of a haul at just the right minute."

"That's so," ejaculated old Captain Dilman, whose singing and honest religious ecstacy had had so profound an effect upon Lem on the night of the Methodist meeting. "I've been around the world three times, and I know such a trick could be played, easy enough."

Everybody looked at the stove during a moment of silence, as if it was a source of ideas; then storekeeper Potts spoke up—

"I never liked that fellow's looks," said he. "Perhaps the Major and Captain's right; that accounts for the awful face Lem always had when he thought nobody was looking at him. There seemed to be something awful on his mind—remorse, like enough, for destroying so much property as a good steamboat amounts to."

"And for killin' his father," suggested a countryman, who was caressing the stove-pipe.

"Oh, yes!—of course—I forgot that," said the merchant. "No wonder he looked as he did. And who knows how many counterfeits he gave out in change from the Squire's store?"

"Guess the Squire wouldn't cry much if he knew it," muttered a man upon whom the Squire had recently foreclosed a chattel mortgage. One or two men laughed. Mr. Potts put on a deprecatory expression, but took care to say nothing in defense of his rival.

" I never *did* believe in sudden conversions," remarked a good, kind-hearted Presbyterian. "Here 'twas told all around town a month or two ago that that boy had been born again—now look at him!"

"There's counterfeit conversions, as well as counterfeit money," retorted the Methodist ex-sailor, with considerable warmth. "That peddler's wagon that gave short weights all around the county a year ago, was druv' by a Presbyterian in good standin'. *My* belief is that Lem was only playin' possum when he made out that he'd gave himself to Jesus. If the Squire hadn't set him agin' him so, like enough he'd have jined the Presbyterians—*then* what 'd you have got off about sudden conversions?"

"Mail open!" shouted the postmaster, in time to prevent these right-hearted champions from contending any longer for the faith as it was delivered unto themselves.

An hour later the conversation above had been welded into the symmetrical statement that Lem had come to Mount Zion for the express purpose of issuing counterfeit money; that he had, with malice aforethought, destroyed the steamboat, and killed his own father during the excitement, to escape recognition by the parent who had tracked him everywhere in the hope of reclaiming him; then, his peculiar expression was due to remorse— that he had shammed conversion, that he had passed much bad money in change from behind the Squire's counter, and that the Squire had winked at the operation.

The news reached the Squire through his own pastor, who earnestly begged a denial of the imputation against his parishioner's honesty, and received one, couched in language so positive that it made him shudder and hurry away. The Squire's eyes flashed fire for a few minutes; then he lapsed into his accustomed religious melancholy, and started for his supper.

"What's wrong with you now, and why wasn't you home to dinner?" was the greeting the Squire received at his own kitchen door.

"I was busy at dinner time," said the Squire, "and— O, Marg'ret, this is an awful wicked world!"

"You haven't been trustin' no other good-for-nothin' that's died without enough to pay his debts, I hope," exclaimed Mrs. Barkum.

"No, Marg'ret, I haven't," replied the Squire, with considerable peevishness, "an' it ain't fair for you to be all the time throwin' that one case up to me—every other storekeeper has done that twenty times. But Lem 's turned out a counterfeiter!"

"An' passed some bad money on you?" asked Mrs. Barkum, setting down her teacup. "I never thought *you'd* get caught at——"

"Oh! no, Marg'ret," groaned the Squire, "what makes you snatch me up so? I haven't took in a counterfeit for a year. But they *do* say that he smashed up that steamboat himself—it was insured in the Illinois Mutual, too, where we have to participate in ev'ry loss; an' that he helped kill his father, an' made-believe got religion, an' passed counterfeit money in makin' change at my store."

"Has any of it been swore back on you?" asked Mrs. Barkum.

"No," said the Squire.

"Then I wouldn't believe a word of it," said Mrs. Barkum. "Besides," said the good lady, poising a spoonful of apple-sauce in mid-air, " 'twouldn't cost *you* anything if he *had* done it."

The Squire groaned, and hurriedly whispered "sh—h —h!" Slowly, however, he seemed to realize that his wife had spoken the truth, and his face exhibited a resigned expression, and then indicated considerable satisfaction, as he exclaimed:

" I do declare, Marg'ret, you *have* got a head for business. You've hit it, even if any of the bad money should be traced to the store. But just isn't it a special providence that we didn't take him again when he came back from Sam Reeves? Time an' again I felt as if it would

13

be only just an' merciful to hire him again, but somethin' inside of me kep' sayin' 'don't do it.'   I didn't
once imagine 'twas a voice from heaven.   I actually kept
thinkin', over an' over, that it was the selfish instincts
of a depraved nature, like all men's got.   I hope I didn't
grieve the Holy Spirit by such misunderstandin'."

"*I* hope," said Mrs. Barkum, laying down her knife
and fork with an imposing crash, "that you didn't commit the unpardonable sin.   'Tain't no small matter, layin'
the doin's of God to your own sinful nature.   What *are*
you thinkin' about, starin' out of the window that way,
Squire?—what *are* you scribblin' with a lead pencil for?"

The Squire did not answer for a moment; then he
said:

"Lem was in an' around the store for nine weeks;
'sposin' he made change only once a day, which is a
small average, an' only gave out a single bad dollar each
time, I'm fifty-four dollars ahead.   Let's give it to the
Lord, Marg'ret—it ain't right to keep such money; an'
if we subscribe it to some benevolent society, it'll bring
us trade.   An' the Lord'll——"

"Why, what's the man thinkin' about?" exclaimed
Mrs. Barkum.   "If Lem gave out a bad bill, makin'

change for you, don't you 'spose he took a good one out of your money-drawer to pay for it? *You* don't make anything by it—don't you see?"

The Squire dropped his head in his hands. " Oh, dear me," he exclaimed, "why didn't I see that before? Now if anybody should swear a bill back on me, 'twould be a dead loss. We took him out of charity, Marg'ret, an' if we lose anything by him, charity ought to pay for it. Seein' that such a matter *may* come up, let's cut off our subscriptions to the Bible Society an' everything else, an' mebbe we'll get through without any loss. I wish I *could* let the Lord's business alone, so he could tend to it himself—I always blunder at it."

CHAPTER XXII.

WESTERN COURTS AND WESTERN JUSTICE.

LEM galloped along toward New Philadelphia, not so much from fear of the officers of the law as of Hixton. He saw from the bluff overhanging the river bottoms, the steamboat round up to the front of the warehouse which constituted the principal part of New Philadelphia, and he quickened his pace. He threw his bridle over one of the pins of a horse-rick in front of the warehouse, and was stepping upon the steamboat's plank, when he felt a hand on his shoulder; looking quickly around, he beheld the Sheriff from Mount Zion. Lem turned pale, and then red, while the Sheriff said:

"I wasn't looking for you, but I guess I'd better take you along. I've got your boss."

"Hixton?" screamed Lem.

"Ah, *that's* the secret, is it?" exclaimed the Sheriff. "Well, I'm sorry for *you*, if you *did* break your word."

"I didn't," said Lem, with considerable indignation, "I——"

"Stop, my boy," said the Sheriff; "I'm not prosecuting attorney, and I don't want to be a witness against you. Don't say a word that'll commit you, unless you do it to your own lawyer—that's my advice. But you're going to have a hard row to hoe. And I've got an unpleasant duty to perform, which the quicker it's done the better." So saying, the Sheriff slipped a pair of handcuffs upon Lem's wrists, led him to his horse, and placed him thereon. Then he whistled to one of his deputies, who came from the warehouse, and with whom he held a whispered consultation, after which he mounted his own horse and led Lem's toward the village of Mount Zion, seven miles distant. When the Sheriff was well out of sight, his assistant started, leading a horse upon which sat Mr. Binkle, his hands fastened behind his back, and his feet strapped under the saddle. Arrived at Mount Zion the Sheriff put Lem into an upper chamber, and Mr. Binkle into the single cell of the jail.

The regular session of the county court, which opened on the first day of the following week, had no lack of business before it. Cases of assault and battery, petty larceny, neighborhood quarrels, suits for large amounts of money, and other cases peculiar to the dockets of courts in new countries, were numerous, but the grand jury knew its business, and quickly found a bill of indictment against Lemuel Pankett for conspiring with Martin Luther Binkle, and other persons unknown to the court, to emit, utter, circulate, pass and exchange imitations of the notes of banking institutions in good repute. About the same time it was whispered about the town that Mr. Binkle had turned State's evidence against the remainder of the gang. The county pulse was up to fever heat; by mutual consent the attorneys in the cases on the calendar for the next day made excuse, so an hour after the court opened, the clerk shouted:

"The State *vs.* Pankett."

The populace had evidently anticipated some such accommodating arrangement for an early trial, for the room was crowded. Men stood in the window sills, and crowded the Judge more closely than was comfortable, while among the lawyers, in front of the jury box, and directly facing the prisoner, on a chair considerately placed for him by a deputy who owed him considerable money, sat Squire Barkum. The good man's mind was too severely overborne by sorrow to admit of his being idly curious: he leaned back in his chair and looked out of the window, behind the Judge, into the clouds—looking, as he afterward said, to see if he could find out where sin originated, and consequently, like most human beings who meddle with things above their comprehension, looking in the wrong direction.

"Lemuel Pankett! Lemuel Pankett! Lemuel Pankett!" shouted the Sheriff; "come into court!"

The crowd near the door opened, and in a moment Lem, escorted by his late companion at cards and tobacco, Deputy-Sheriff Turner, was conducted to the prisoner's box. Everybody leaned forward and enjoyed a good stare, while the prisoner dropped his eyes, and his face flushed. Good Squire Barkum stood up, adjusted his glasses, and looked reproachfully at the prisoner, noticing which, Lem held up his head and stared defiantly. The sorrowful old man groaned and sat down.

A jury was soon empaneled; the only question propounded to any juryman by Bill Fussell, who had volunteered as Lem's counsel, being as to whether he had within six months received any counterfeit bank-notes which he believed had been brought into the county by the accused or any supposed accomplices. Numerous witnesses were called, and established the fact that they had received counterfeits, mostly large notes, which had in every case been traced to Lem Pankett.

Finally the clerk said:

"Call Martin Luther Binkle."

"Martin Luther Binkle! Martin Luther Binkle! Martin Luther Binkle! come into court!" shouted the Sheriff.

Mr. Binkle soon appeared, assisted by a deputy; his handcuffs were removed, and he took the witness-chair as if it was his customary lounging-place, winked at his own lawyer, bowed to the judge, rubbed his hands, and looked about him with an air of general proprietorship. When the oath was administered, he kissed the book with a hearty smack, as if he enjoyed the operation; and but for a temporary cloud which passed over his brow as he noticed something apparently unpleasing in the gallery, he seemed a good-natured, wide-awake business man.

"Mr. Binkle," said the prosecuting attorney, "do you know Lemuel Pankett, the prisoner at the bar?"

"Yes, sir."

"How long?"

"A few days—about a fortnight, say."

"Have you ever known him to have counterfeit money in his possession?"

" Yes, sir."

" How much, or how much at a time?"

" Off and on, perhaps a thousand dollars—three hundred dollars on one single occasion."

"You know the money was counterfeit?"

" Yes, sir."

" How?"

"Because I'm an expert in that sort of thing—I supplied it to him myself."

" Had he any accomplices?"

Mr. Binkle looked at his counsel; the lawyer frowned.

" I decline to answer that question," said Mr. Binkle. " Under my arrangement with the authorities, I am only bound to give such evidence as will criminate the prisoner."

" Do you know whether he spent any of these counterfeits?" asked the prosecutor.

"Yes, sir, he did."

" How do you know?"

"Because he hadn't a da—hadn't a cent when I first saw him, and was half crazy because he hadn't. I gave him a twenty-dollar counterfeit, and in an hour he was back with a bottle of liniment, and nineteen dollars in money."

" Any other cases?"

" I gave him three hundred dollars in counterfeits one day, and in twenty-four hours he was back with three good horses and nearly a hundred and fifty dollars in good money."

"Did anybody else give him any bad money to spend?"

"Yes, sir—my partner."

" What's his name?"

"May it please your honor," exclaimed ex-Judge Compston, Binkle's attorney, springing to his feet, " I object to the witness answering that question. The law holds that the mere possession of counterfeit money is a misdemeanor, and punishable to the full extent of the law, made to cover the worst cases of counterfeiting. The witness has established this. I object to the putting to him of any irrelevant questions."

"'Tain't the fair thing to play on a gentleman, in an up-and-down business transaction," remarked the witness, looking around him for sympathy.

"The witness will be quiet," said the Judge, "and the prosecuting attorney must be bound by the agreement which was made by the State with the witness."

"Cross-examine," said the prosecutor, dropping sulkily into his chair. Bill Fussell arose and addressed the witness :

"Do you believe the prisoner knew the money you gave him was counterfeit?"

"No."

"Why?"

"Because I wouldn't have a man shove queer money for me after he knew what it was—it takes all business ways right out of him."

"What was he doing at New Philadelphia for you?"

"Nothing."

"What were *you* doing there?"

"Waiting for a boat to take me out of the country."

"What for?"

"I thought some of the counterfeits would be found out pretty soon, I'd got off such a lot of them through him.

"Was he going with you?"

"No."

"Why?"

"Because I hadn't asked him to, he didn't know I was going, and I wouldn't have had him with me if he'd wanted to go."

"Why not?"

"Because he'd found out what my business was."

"How did he find out?"

"Bill——"

A pistol-shot startled the court, and the witness fell out of his chair, bleeding profusely from the chest. Every one, the Judge included, sprang up, and the Judge shouted, "Mr. Sheriff! preserve order!" but the Sheriff hurried to the side of the wounded man, and whispered:

"Bill Hixton?"

"The Bible—quick!" gasped the witness. "As I hope to be saved from hell, the boy never had a notion of what we were up to, and was trying to run away from *us* when he was caught. I acknowledge the Lord Jesus Christ to be——"

The witness' voice failed him. His face twitched into agonized lines, every one of which was eloquent, but nobody could read them. By a violent effort he recovered his voice, and gasped:

"A man that—the boy—loved and helped—told him: he—was the only—only friend the boy—ever had, if—if he was a—horse-thief. I'm dying—trusting only in the —merits of—Jesus Christ——"

"Shocking!" exclaimed Squire Barkum.

"It's what *you'll* say when you die, isn't it, you old scoundrel?" said Bill Fussell, confronting the Squire.

"Mr. Sheriff, you *must* keep order," said the judge. "Who else will the prosecution call?"

"Nobody," said the prosecuting attorney, as the Sheriff shouted "Order!" with great vigor, and sent deputies in search of the murderer.

"Will the defense call any one?"

"No, your honor—we rest," said Bill Fussell, "and trust to the good sense of the jury."

The jurymen looked at each other, and exchanged some rapid words; the foreman stood up, and exclaimed:

"Not Guilty!"

"Order! gentlemen," shouted the clerk. "Gentlemen of the jury, arise and look upon the prisoner; prisoner, arise——"

But a tempest of cheers drowned the voice of the clerk—everybody crowded around Lem to shake hands, some of the jurymen jumping from their benches to participate. The court-room was nearly emptied as Lem, leaning upon Bill Fussell, walked out, apparently with some difficulty. The Sheriff sent for the coroner and his own horse, the former to sit upon Binkle, and the latter for himself to sit upon as he took part in the chase after the murderer. But a hero, who had emerged from the clutch of the law, was greater in the eyes of the public than either a dead counterfeiter or a live ruffian — so most of the village followed Lem, or broke into groups and talked about him.

CHAPTER XXIII.

IN WHICH THE HERO ESCAPES FROM THE ROAD.

LEM and his counsel walked slowly down the main street of the village. Storekeepers and their customers hurried out of stores to shake hands with Lem and congratulate him. To every one Lem said "Thank you," but he did not seem to be as greatly elated as a man who had barely escaped State prison should be. As the couple passed along a stretch of broad fence from behind which no smiling friends approached, the young lawyer said:

"Cheer up, cheer up, little chap—you act as if I was the Sheriff. What's the matter?"

Lem groaned. "Oh, lots of things," he said. "I haven't got any money to give *you*, for one thing."

"Wipe that out, then," said the lawyer. "I'd have given *you* a fifty, poor as I am, for the chance of defending you if I'd known how the case was going to turn out. It'll do me more good on the circuit to have been your counsel in this case than all the work I've ever done before.   What else is on your mind?"

"The old thing," sighed Lem.   "Out of work again. Everybody's makin' a fuss over me to-day, but you'd see how they'd scatter if I'd ask any of 'em for a job."

The lawyer looked down compassionately, almost disdainfully, at the pinched face, glassy eyes and bent back of the figure beside him.

"Look here, Lem," said he; "you're no more fit to work than a tom-cat is to take hold of an equity case. *That's* the reason people don't hire you."

"I *am*, too," declared Lem, growing straighter and fuller in the face, and brighter-eyed for a moment.   "Or I was," said he, catching his breath and dropping back into his old stoop again.

"You were, before that infernal old Squire took you up and worked you out," said Bill Fussell.   "It's an infernal shame that a church member like he is, with plenty of money, should work the life and soul right out of a man.   I've been blazing mad about it a hundred times."

"Nobody prevented him," said Lem.

The young lawyer's complexion deepened from its

habitual carmine to a hue almost purple. "Yes," said he, "and I was one of the people that kept their mouths shut. What's everybody's business is nobody's business. I'm going right across the street and have it out with the old scoundrel—and myself."

"Don't, please don't," said Lem, clutching the lawyer's arm tightly. "Help me down to Myvy's, where I used to stay—I can never get there alone."

"Why, what do you want to go to that dirty hole for?" asked the lawyer.

"They think enough of me to trust me for my board," said Lem—"nobody else does."

"But you'll have to live like a hog there," said the lawyer, "and you need to be taken care of. Myvy's a drunken beast, and his wife's the dirtiest looking woman in town; they never have anything unless they steal it, I guess."

"They were always kind to me," said Lem; "nobody else was, even if they stole what they had."

"Go back to Ben Ringsell's," said the young lawyer, turning purple again; "I'll pay your board for a month, and I'll find you something to do—somebody's *got* to give you a job."

14

The couple had just passed the post office, when out
rushed the postmaster. "Hurrah for you, Lem!" said
he. "Glad to see you out. Here's a letter for you."

"From mother!" said Lem, looking two or three
years younger very suddenly. "No, it ain't," he continued, his countenance falling. "Who else wants to
send me a letter?"

"Maybe you could find out by breaking it open,"
suggested the lawyer.

Lem acted upon the advice of his counsel, and took
from the envelope two fifty dollar notes and a scrap torn
from a newspaper margin; upon this latter was scrawled,
in pencil, the following message:

"{Rum a nuther uv old binkuls korpsiZ. tak kare oV
yewwer muthar. damm binkul keep a Stif uper lip.
moar a kummen."

Lem's face was blankness itself as he handed the letter
to the lawyer.

"No signature," said Bill Fussell. "What's the post-
mark?—New Philadelphia, eh? Hello, this envelope's
been turned; perhaps the inside will throw some light
on the subject." The lawyer tore open the ends of the
envelope, and read, from the inside of the back: "Thomas
Lodge; what post-office is this? he is addressed—"

Lem snatched the envelope, tore it into a thousand pieces, threw it into the mud and trampled upon it. Bill Fussell looked surprised and said:

" Why, don't you want to know where your friends hang out their shingles?"

" No," said Lem, " I don't want to do nothin' but get into a bed somewhere. I can't hardly stand up. Can't you—get one of these changed, so I can send ninety dollars to my mother—right away. I'll keep ten—I feel as if I was goin to be reel sick."

" I'll send it for you," said Fussell; "come along to Ben Ringsell's now."

They started; the lawyer became conscious that Lem leaned heavier and heavier upon his arm. Suddenly Lem's grasp relaxed and he fell upon the pavement in front of Squire Barkum's store. The lawyer placed his new hat under Lem's head, dashed across the street to the hotel, snatched the brandy bottle (whose location he well knew) from before the eyes of the astonished proprietor, and hurried back. Several men appeared suddenly, apparently from nowhere, and from his own front door, behind which he had been watching Lem's approach, and composing a speech congratulatory, conciliatory and scriptural, appeared the Squire himself.

Dr. Beers, who happened just in the nick of time to be riding by, jumped from his carriage, the Squire's pastor emerged from the post-office door followed by the postmaster, while the circuit judge, who had been compelled to adjourn court because of the excitement in the room, came down the street at a most unjudicial pace.

"Stand back, everybody!" exclaimed the doctor. "Air is what he needs."

For two or three minutes there was utter silence; the doctor knelt with his fingers on Lem's pulse, and at last whispered:

"You can't last much longer, Lem."

"I know it," said Lem; "I want to be prayed for."

In an instant good Squire Barkum was upon his knees on the brick pavement. He had got as far as "Almighty God, we thine unworthy—" when the dying man said in a very thin voice, but yet with considerable energy:

"Get up—I don't want *your* prayers—I want some *good* person's."

The Squire's clasped hands fell from their devotional pose, his eye-brows raised, and his lower jaw dropped.

"Get up," repeated Lem. "I don't want anything from anybody that'll listen to you. Oh, God!—I'm killed!"

Again the Squire dropped on his knees, perhaps with some desire to change the subject of his late conversation.

"Who killed you?" asked the old man.

Lem slowly and with great difficulty raised himself on one elbow, fixed his eyes on the Squire, and exclaimed:

"YOU!"

The Squire slowly got upon his feet, fell back, leaned against the front of his store, and gazed into the limbs of a tree on the edge of the sidewalk. The doctor bent his head close to Lem and said:

"You haven't got time to be particular, Lem, but is there anybody you'd particularly like to have pray for you?"

"Yes," whispered Lem, "Bill Hixton."

A murmur ran through the little crowd; somebody elbowed a way through the bystanders and bent over Lem; it was the Sheriff.

"Lem," said he, "you're dying. Bill Hixton's a thief. You know something about him. Don't go into the presence of God with any concealed sin on your conscience. Do you know where Bill Hixton is?"

" Yes."

" Where?"

"Out of your reach," gasped Lem, with a happy smile.

" Who else?" whispered the doctor, after a moment's pause.

" Send for Aunty Bates," whispered Lem.

" She's sick abed," said the doctor.

"Then little Billy Miles," gasped Lem. " Oh—— mother!"—The sick man closed his eyes and went into a court in which there is no danger that the innocent will suffer for the guilty, and in which turning state's evidence will not save scoundrels.

CHAPTER XXIV.

TWO COUPLES OF PENITENTS.

THE inhabitants of Mount Zion were not, as a body, familiar with the course of all human history, or with the habits of the best society, but they had in them one of those qualities of nature which make the world akin, and show that the ancient Greek and the modern negro, the French aristocrat and the New York rowdy, are men of the same blood—they knew how to heap upon a corpse the kind attentions which they had withheld from its owner. Lem's funeral was the finest one which Mount Zion had ever known. The coffin was as superb a thing as the rival cabinet-makers of Mount Zion could turn out between them; the nails had real silver heads, extemporized from five-cent coins by an ingenious inhabitant, and the plate upon the lid made up in ornamental flourishes what the paucity of information current about Lem's age, etc., caused to be lacking in the length of the inscription. The inside was trimmed with fine silk, and in considerable taste, the most high-toned

ladies in the town contending with each other for a share
in the work. The best of the two hearses in the town
was newly varnished, the two cabinet-makers combined
their span of horses, and both gentlemen sat upon the
driver's box. The court adjourned, by request of all the
members of the bar, and the Judge rode in the first
buggy, with the Methodist pastor, who had claimed the
mournful pleasure of officiating, on account of Lem's
probationary membership in his church. In the next
conveyance rode, as chief mourners, little Billy Miles
and Aunty Bates, who had got out of bed for the purpose. Behind them was a buggy in which sat the Sheriff
and Bill Fussell, each in a new shiny hat and a solemn
countenance. After these came everybody in the county,
in buggies, farm wagons, on horse-back and on foot;
some horses carried two riders each, and in an old stage-
coach, looking as disreputable and sad as themselves,
rode the loafers from Micham's rum-shop. The procession was so long that it extended through the entire
length of the main street. After it had turned out toward
the little cemetery, however, a rapidly driven buggy con-
taining the Squire and Mrs. Barkum took a place in the
rear, and followed the others; then a couple of horse-

men, with very clean-shaven faces, short hair, new and badly-fitting black clothes, galloped out of a side road and fell into line behind the Squire's buggy.

"Marg'ret," said the Squire, "the sin of blood-guiltiness is onto us."

"Squire," said Mrs. Barkum, "I know it. It's good we ain't livin' under the old dispensation, where blood had to pay for blood."

"We're worse off than that, Marg'ret," said the Squire. "There's only one thing we *can* atone for it with."

"What's that?" asked the tearful lady.

"Money," groaned the Squire.

"That's so," sighed his wife.

"Lodge," said one of the smoothly-shaved men, "it's awful solemn. I wish I hadn't shot Binkle, almost."

"Sh—h—h!" whispered the other man. "I'll run any risk to follow that boy to the last of him, but I don't want to be throwed away. I wish I was in the hearse with him."

"Don't be a —— fool," replied Hixton. "You helped put him there; you've got to do lots for his old woman before *you'll* stand a chance of layin' comfortable in a hearse."

"That's so," whispered the counterfeiter.

"Marg'ret," said the Squire, "we've got to support the family."

"Let's," said Mrs. Barkum.

"We've got to eddicate the children," continued the Squire.

"I 'spose—we must," said Mrs. Barkum, rubbing her eyes.

"If *we* was in that hearse, Mar—"

"Don't Squire—don't," exclaimed Mrs. Barkum. "I ain't as strong as I used to be."

"If we *was* there, Marg'ret," repeated the Squire, "our money'd go to the county, and nobody knows who'd spend it. Let's give it all to the Lord some way or other while we've got a chance."

"Anything, Squire," sobbed the old lady.

"*We've* got to come to it *some* day," said the counterfeiter to his companion.

"For God's sake don't talk about it," said the horse-thief.

"I only wish we was as good and ready as he was," said Lodge.

" We never *will* be—the miserable little pinched-up, knocked-kneed cuss," said Hixton.

"Let's swear off ev'ry thing," suggested Lodge.

" Agreed," said Hixton. " Shake hands on it. The way the air feels I reckon there's a witness mighty close at hand."

" So do I," said Lodge.

As the cortege reached the little cemetery, it seemed there were not fences enough in the neighborhood to tie all the horses to, and the interior of the cemetery appeared to be a very lively corral. The grave had been dug beside that of Lem's father, and everybody crowded as near to it as possible—everybody but the Squire, his wife, the counterfeiter, and the horse-thief. When the ceremonies were concluded and the people turned to leave the grave, Lodge and Hixton galloped off, as if to dodge the eye of justice, and the Squire drove away rapidly, apparently with the same end in view.

CONCLUSION.

AFTER the villagers had sufficiently discussed the circumstances of Lem's final disappearance, it became slowly evident that a change had taken place in Squire Barkum. He was no less sharp in his bargains than ever, but it was noticed that after he had transacted his business with people who might possibly be in financial straits, he dropped his elbows on the counter, his head on his hands, and pumped them with great persistency. Then it was noised abroad that the Squire had absolutely forced an excellent assortment of groceries, and materials for winter clothing upon the widow Morrow, who had for several years been trying to maintain in comfort three children too small to work, and had failed most pitifully.

Then the village postmaster felt that he violated no bond of secrecy in saying that every week the Squire received a letter, most illegibly addressed, and postmarked with the name of Lem's native village. It was also remarked by the Squire's competitors that about once a week, and nearly every week, the poor old man appeared at their stores in quest of a ten-dollar bill on some eastern bank, and that he objected strongly to using a twenty.

One day a steamboat from Cincinnati dropped in front of one of the Mount Zion warehouses several heavy packages of boxed stone, not entirely concealed. Mount Zion curiosity was aroused, and finally gratified by the sight of a shapely monument over Lem's remains. Upon the four sides of the square shaft were Bible passages, not exactly innumerable, but extremely frequent, and all of them hinting at the salvation and consequent bliss of those who did what they could, and loved much.

Then people heard that the Squire's pastor was very much exercised about the state of his parishioner's mind. The old merchant seemed first inclined to pick flaws in the doctrine of vicarious atonement, and then to substitute Lem Pankett for the sacred person whose atoning merits he had previously made the excuse for all his own sins. The Squire, too, had become possessed of the idea that he had committed the unpardonable sin. The clergyman combatted the notion, until, during an unexpected logical spasm, it struck him that the Squire was rather happier with the idea of going to hell than he had previously been with his hope of heaven; so he left the Squire in the enjoyment of his fears, and devoted his energies to the task of encouraging the old man to make the best possible use of his remaining time and large property.

As for the remaining good people at Mount Zion, some of them followed the Squire afar off, and some of them made haste to be blind and deaf, lest they should open their hearts and pockets and be born again. The results of Lem's death were as good as could have been expected, when one thinks of how little, in comparison with their gigantic possibilities, the life and death of the Man of Sorrows accomplished. But some men saw that if the poor were not helped for God's sake, they *would* be Satan's, and that, in the latter event the church and society would both have to suffer, while no one reaped any benefit. So, for the sake of their pockets, some hard heads and harder hearts took a share in the work which, for humanity's sake only, they would never have touched.

THE END.